ALWAYS a DANCER

A MEMOIR

....
ROBERT BRASSEL

RESOURCE *Publications* • Eugene, Oregon

Resource Publications
A division of Wipf and Stock Publishers
199 W 8th Ave, Suite 3
Eugene, OR 97401

Always a Dancer
A Memoir
By Brassel, Robert
Copyright © 2006 by Brassel, Robert All rights reserved.
Softcover ISBN-13: 978-1-7252-6746-6
Hardcover ISBN-13: 978-1-7252-6748-0
eBook ISBN-13: 978-1-7252-6747-3
Publication date 2/11/2020
Previously published by AAD Distributing, 2006

Dedication

To Linda and Matthew

Contents

1	A Gift Identified
7	Inspiration
13	A Father at Home
19	Looking for Lessons
25	New York City
32	Professional Training
41	A Contract/Surprises
49	A Grateful Soldier
64	My Way Back
74	Falling in Love Again, For Real
94	A Major Change
102	On My Own

112	A Most Extraordinary Tour
131	Dancing Together
138	The Road to London
147	A 'Beauty' in Beautiful South Africa
163	Hiatus
172	Getting on with It
177	The Dance Academy
187	Life after Plies
194	A Second Career
202	The Gift of Music
210	A Thickening Waistline
221	A Knock on the Door
226	Results

and

EPILOGUE

Acknowledgements

To the many people who, over the years, have suggested, encouraged and insisted that I write my story, I am grateful to have seen their day, and mine, finally come to pass. To Connie Micarelli who introduced me to self- publishing and to James Micarelli who proof read the manuscript, I offer my special appreciation. I am grateful to Shayna Loeffler for her fine work on the book's cover design and to Phil Schaffer for his detailed insight into the final manuscript. Finally, to my wife Linda, who lovingly advised and consented and to my son, Matthew, who patiently improved my computer skills, I love and thank them both for being a very big part of my story.

A Gift Identified

I don't remember a time when I did not want to move to the sound of music. I have always been a dancer. I have always thought about dancing.

If this was a vocation, then I followed that interest. If this was a calling, I heard the call loud and clear. Innate self identification signaled who I was. Dance ability has been the backbone of my self-esteem. I feel very fortunate for having had just this piece of fate on my plate, not to mention the story about to unfold.

As a family we would not have a normal existence. Our Father was not a 9am-5pm, five day a week working father. We would not be a small family continuously raised in the same cozy suburb. Instead our lives would resemble a touring ballet company. Our only constant was a loving Mother who was always caring while we grew in size and number. Father was a traveling salesman. He drove North, South, East and West of these United States in his efforts to develop the Encyclopedia Americana branch offices. Mother was intent on being with him. It was not expected to be long-enduring, certainly not sixteen years in which she would give birth to a total of seven children.

Our family was composed of four girls and three boys. The birth order was girl, boy, boy, twins (boy and girl), girl, girl. I was the third child. As the children grew in size and number, the towns and cities continued to change. Each Encyclopedia Americana branch took several months to get up and running before we were off to another area. Our education was sometimes in two or three states in a single year. Eventually Mother did not entirely unpack. She knew it would not be long before we would again move on. It became clear that this pattern would not change until and if my Father became a corporate head of the company. Not all of us thrived in this atmosphere but I could not get enough of life.

Children can make friends for a lifetime in a singe day. It

appeared that acclimating for most of us was not traumatic. Our constant caregiver, my Mother, did not change. However, this nomadic lifestyle offered its share of arguments between my parents. Mother was concerned that she was losing contact with her family. Both of my parents were born and raised in Chicago, Illinois. An indication for her desire to return there was that she managed to give birth to each of her first three children in Chicago. My birth was perhaps her closest call. On the day before I was born, she decided to leave Long Beach, California with my elder brother and sister in tow. Against doctor's orders, she boarded a train bound for Chicago. Her contractions began an hour outside of the city. I was born at Children's Hospital thirty minutes after the train arrived in Chicago.

Thereafter, she wondered if she ever would be "settled". Only a life changing event could change the pattern. For the time being there was much work for my Father to do and he was being very successful at it.

So many children! During the 1940's and 1950's birth control basically consisted of inferior condoms. Large families were common. What was uncommon was the constant moving. Military families did this regularly though they generally had smaller families, staying in one place for thirteen months at a time.

It is from Lincoln, Nebraska, that I have my earliest memory. Interestingly enough, it was not dancing but rolling downhill inside an automobile tire. My five year old brother Murphy would chart my path after he had fitted me into the tire. It was up to me to get out when the ride was over, wherever that happened to be. In later years when I spoke of this recollection, my Mother informed me that I was then two and a half years old. She was too pregnant with twins to do much about my brother's pranks.

What she would also relay to me was the fact that whenever she had the radio music playing, I was particularly content. She did that a lot, especially after the birth of the twins, because I managed to keep myself engrossed in the music. It was not until kindergarten that I remembered dancing to it.

From Lincoln to Hollywood, Long Beach to San Francisco, Tampa to Fort Lauderdale, Jacksonville to Topeka, to Denver and on and on we traveled!

I became enamored with traveling; automobiles, trains and sometimes airplanes. I liked the trains the best because I had lots of freedom on them. Though I discovered several cars at once, I never got lost for long. I always came back excepting for the harrowing two days in Denver when I decided to show new friends, visiting from Chicago, our new city of Denver. My friends were twins, a boy and a girl. We were all three and a half years old.

Managing to escape the chattering adults, we left the white

picket fence gate. We were found by a woman who lived alone. Two days later she called the police to retrieve us. It appeared as though she wanted to keep us and then changed her mind. Local news reports had all of Denver involved. Having heard the retelling of the incident many times, I could sympathize with the parents, particularly Mother who had a new set of twins to take care of bringing her total number of children to five. Once again one is reminded of the particular difficulties children bring along with their mostly smiling existence.

All families experience life more or less through "events" created by their children. In our family these "events" were in the transitional state. They did not happen in the same city or home often. We often recollected events differently from each other. One of us would insist that it was in Jacksonville where eighteen month old twins, Danny and Diane, rollicked with the alligators in the backyard swamp; onetime nearly becoming lunch when one of them tried to retrieve a ball. Another would insist that the alligator incident happened in Fort Lauderdale because Jacksonville was where the sixth child of the family, Bonnie Sue, fell off the balcony when she was a toddler. Luckily, her head landed at the apex of a chair leg and the cement, greatly cushioning her fall. She survived to be her beautiful self. Then Judy, the eldest, would tell of a Christmas morning in Topeka when I opened everyone's presents before they woke up (I was under the age of reason!).

Murphy, the next eldest, would talk of the time I was his chauffeur and took the car backwards down the driveway hill, ending up inches from the neighbor's front door across the street. He said that happened in Los Angeles but Judy and I were sure that it occurred in Tampa. Then Mother usually settled the matter with an anecdote that related to another matter of adult concern that had happened at the same time.

Father was often absent from these "events." In fact, he was absent a whole lot of the time. Mother was really raising the family alone. I think her serious sense of loneliness was established during this time. There wasn't time to meet people or to get to know neighbors. She was on a solo mission: to settle down where she could have a normal life. Her deep love for my Father was the catalyst for such lasting commitment. She believed that one day it would be a different life. She wanted to have her marriage in tact to go along with it. Meanwhile, what she did have was the ongoing "events" provided by her children.

Inspiration

One "event" that everyone agreed upon was the day I came home from kindergarten class with a note. The city was Topeka, Kansas. On the note was written "DOROTHY THOMPSON SCHOOL OF DANCING" along with a telephone number. My classmate Johnny had his mother write the note for me just as I had asked. Johnny regularly left kindergarten class early on Tuesdays. I asked him where he went. Kindergarten was okay but whenever we had to join in a circle and perform "Ring around the Rosy" I was bothered by the sound of the piano.

Like a bad smell, it was probably very out of tune. That is always when Johnny got to leave. I was quite anxious to escape with him.

Johnny revealed that he went off to dancing school on Tuesdays. If this was anything like what I had been doing to the radio music at home, then I could go to dancing school too! Mother was not surprised when I handed her the note. She knew music made me move. However, it would be some time before she acted on my request to join Johnny's dancing class. I tugged at her dress daily. I was too young to consider her special complications in arranging to get me there. She was without a car and would have to ask a neighbor, whom she did not know, for the favor. Finally, one wonderful Tuesday afternoon we arrived to meet Mrs. Thompson.

A crowded reception area needed to be negotiated before one could actually see what one was hearing from the main studio. There in the middle of all the dancers was a teenage girl dancing on roller skates while playing the accordion and singing! I was totally captivated. When the number finished, Mrs. Thompson yelled out for the little boy at the doorway to come front and center. Pointing to me, she waved me into the room.

"How old are you, young man? What is your name? Is your Mommy here? Let me show you something that I want you to do. Follow me." She began a "Shuffle Off to Buffalo."

routine complete with a ball change tap rhythm which I easily followed. She asked me to repeat it with a top hat and cane, beating the cane on the ball change rhythm every third beat rather than fourth. Then she asked me to do it alone. Finally, she asked her multi-talented daughter (the teenager who had made the big impression), to retrieve my Mother from the reception area. Mrs. Thompson asked us to join her in her office, giving the cast of her annual recital a ten minute break.

Mrs. Thompson explained to Mother that she was fond of typecasting. It was the only way to get what one really wanted onto the stage. Johnny was already cast in the leading part that she had just worked on with me. When she saw me at the doorway, she saw the "look" she was after. She went on to explain that, though most children mimic well, she was quite taken with my sense of rhythm at the get go. I was the boy she wanted for the part. She would take care of matters with Johnny and his mother. She was also generous in offering me my first dance scholarship right there in Topeka, Kansas. It was 1949 and all was right with the world.

All was not right with Johnny's mother. My mother found that things were happening too quickly. She had been viewing brochures while I was having the first audition of my career! Of course what had just transpired was not fair to Johnny. The performing arts were not bound to fairness of any sort; nonetheless Mrs. Thompson was not nearly as successful with Johnny's mother as she had been with my mother. In fact, when Mother heard of the chaos caused by Mrs. Thompson's decision, she was set to back out of the offer. Mrs. Thompson quickly worked matters out, making sure that both boys would dance the part during the three- performance run. I would dance opening night and Johnny would dance the other two performances.

The following six weeks were heaven sent. I believe that then and there I knew what I was going to do in my life. I would have a dance career. I would be always a dancer!

As fate would have it, my father moved the family to Akron, Ohio, ten days before opening night. Johnny performed opening night and the second and third performances as well. Alas! All was fair for Johnny. Mrs. Thompson had a last meeting with Mother and me. She reminded Mother to keep me in dancing. With a smile and a wink in her eye she looked at me, "He enjoys it so."

And so went my first encounter with another person who seemed to know exactly what I knew about dancing: its wonder. Being in class and rehearsal with other students was akin to having fun the way my brother did with sports activities. This was satisfying and fulfilling. My young age did not seem to play a role in how I felt about moving in space with music. Nothing about that has ever changed.

Mine was going to be an inspired life. It was also going to be years before I would again step inside of a dance studio. My

Father did not want me to study dance. His attitude was very clear. He did not understand dancing lessons for boys and he wanted no part of a conversation that headed in that direction. Still there was between us a strong passion, one we both understood. It was a passion for life. I imagined that he secretly knew how I felt and in time would be proud of me. My thoughts would come closer to reality every time he saw Fred Astaire on television and called me to the TV set. We did not talk about Astaire or dancing. We just had silent time watching together. I decided to no longer ask for lessons. I was about to learn what it was to persevere by "choreographing" my own lessons to the radio music in the basement.

The next few years saw a steady development in Father's business growth, now neck and neck with the Encyclopedia Britannica Corporation. This was largely due to my Father's efforts. Upon the untimely death of the company president, my father was rewarded with that position. At 43, he became the youngest president in the company's history.

Mother saw what she had long been looking for; a settled future. First there would be one last move. Upstate New York was the last area to be developed. The main office was set up in Buffalo. By this time we had Deborah Leigh, the family's seventh child, with us. My Father liked to say he had a child for every day of the week. Starting with Sunday that would make me Tuesday! The eldest sibling, Judy, was not happy about being Sunday, the first born. In fact she wasn't happy about having so many children in the family, period. She felt the responsibility was more than she could handle. Still, in general, things were looking up for all of us. We were then a complete family, all the time.

A Father at Home

We were getting used to having my Father with us all the time. He was getting used to being a "hands on" Father. Life was busier. Salesmen, and often their families, visited at the house regularly. They were to become a mainstay, almost like an extended family. By June of 1955, we moved into 211 Lamarck Drive in the town of Snyder, New York. The large home had an equally large lot attached to it. Father planned for a swimming pool to be built on it. Mother hired help for the house. She seemed much happier now that the traveling had stopped.

With my siblings and/or friends from school, I was dancing in the basement daily. We had a full size jukebox in the basement. We danced to whatever was on it. I was beginning to sense that there was more to dancing than I knew about, something akin to technique or method that I was missing. Was it what they taught at dancing schools?

While listening to the radio announcer one afternoon, I learned that the prize for answering a question correctly was free ballroom dancing lessons at Arthur Murray's Studio. After winning the prize, I wondered how I would be able to get to the lessons. I was eleven years old. With the help of my sister Judy's boyfriend, I arrived for the first lesson. I was learning the cha-cha with adults. Here was a structure, a method of learning steps on counts to rhythm: that familiar captivation from Mrs. Thompson's studio. After a couple more lessons and several different dances learned, the studio manager asked if I would be interested in working with the "Cotillion" program in the afternoons. Would I like to teach other adolescents what I had learned?

It was out of the question given my age, school status and lack of regular transportation into downtown Buffalo. Again, my Mother was not surprised that I had found a dancing school. Again, my Father was not amused. However, the lessons signaled what my dancing was missing. Training would be essential to my development. I could not see how I would get consistent training. The obstacles were too many. I knew it would be later on, somehow, that I would find my way into a dance studio on a regular basis. For the time being, I needed to become closer with my Father.

Sitting at the dining room table watching my Father do the books for his business was a fascinating experience for me. Without the aid of a calculator, he would repeatedly scan down a column of numbers, putting a figure at the bottom. He did this with great speed. I would try to catch him in error. I never did. During these sessions, he would speak with me about his plans for the house, pool completion, and that he and Mother would be going to Hawaii for their twentieth anniversary the following September. The warmth of his personality and the largess of his thinking captured my imagination. I felt very close to him, as though I understood this man that I had known for such a short period of my life. I thought he was stupendous! I wanted to spend much more time with him.

It was a wish that would be unfulfilled. In the early morning hours of August 23, 1956, Father had his third heart attack. He died on August 25th. Suddenly the family's future was changed from hopeful to doubtful. At 39 years of age and pregnant with her eighth child, Mother's reaction to her loss was so great that she was hospitalized for two weeks following the funeral. This resulted in a miscarriage of the baby.

We seven children were between the ages of three and sixteen. Murphy was now the "head" of the family. Understandably, his reaction was akin to a deer with headlights aimed right at him. He seemed to turn off. Judy's devastation took the form of an additional work schedule. With that and her being a junior in High School, she was around as little as possible. What she had feared most was happening. Would she now be straddled with responsibility? Was she left holding the bag? Both she and Murphy cushioned me, being blessed with my placement in the family order. I took responsibility for the younger ones. At least I could help keep an eye on them.

Murphy took a job at the local super market, lying about his age. I shoveled driveways every weekend. In Buffalo, winter lasted from November through March. Thus, the three of us could help Mother with money. She would need it. The corporation gave her only six months severance pay. That and Social Security was all the money she had. A $50,000 life insurance policy from Prudential Life was approved, but the check for the first premium payment was found in a stamped envelope on my Father's desk three weeks after he died. I clearly remember the insurance agent coming to the house. He sadly explained that, had the envelope even been postmarked, the company would have paid the benefit.

As feelings of sadness permeated everything we did, I was also beginning to feel a weight being lifted from me. Though I was not clear about this, I realized later what it meant. For the first time, I could seriously think of dancing as my future career without the obstacle of my Father's resistance. Of course, I could not think of lessons at a time like that. Still, I was feeling lighter than air itself.

When Mother came home from the hospital, we were all anxious to see what her direction would be. She had the choice to stay in Buffalo or return to her roots in the Midwest. She decided to have five of us spend the fall with her sister, Martha, in Black River Falls, Wisconsin. She kept Judy and my youngest sister Deborah Leigh with her while she sold the house and looked for a smaller, more affordable one. She said she wanted to stay put. It was where her husband was buried.

Many questioned her decision, even those friends and neighbors whom we did not know well. All were of like thinking; she should have help with her family. Aunt Martha was welcoming. She wanted us to be with her. She was clear about Mother not being able to manage alone.

Twenty years had passed since she and Father had left Chicago to build a life and family together. Now, facing the age of forty, she was uncertain of what it would be like for her to return to the Midwest. Everyone had moved on, developed their own families and was in a very different place and time in their lives. For the first time, Mother had a sense of being settled. She had remained in the same city for more than two years. Her children were well ensconced in their various schools and social activities; settled in the "permanent" way children tend to do so easily.

Finally, the man she loved and cherished was buried in Buffalo. At that point in time she was not able to leave him there. As time would prove, Mother was a one-man woman who remained widowed for the rest of her life.

Looking for Lessons

Returning from Wisconsin, we were a fatherless family but a family together again. Our three-bedroom home was only a couple of blocks from our former house. We felt secure in Snyder. We had our friends and our school activities there.

    I began developing my choreography in a different manner. It involved more people. Because I was known as "the dancer," many of my Gamma Phi Sigma fraternity brothers in high school wanted to learn how to dance with the girls. At slumber parties, I would oblige them. They were very grateful. Remembering that period, I am still struck by the guy who feels uncomfortable moving on the dance floor. I would help out anybody.

Variety shows, operettas and local theatrical productions were always on the lookout for male dancers. I went to as many tryouts as I could and I did as many shows as I had time for. This, in addition to dance championships for the city and state, developed my reputation quickly. By my junior year in high school, I was confident enough about dancing that I auditioned for the University of Buffalo's professional production of Cole Porter's "Kiss Me Kate."

The National Ballet of Canada was on an extended layoff. Their male dancers came down from Toronto for the audition. There were twenty professionals and me. The audition was for four men to work in the "Too Darn Hot" number, made famous in the film version by Shirley MacLaine. I followed every combination that the choreographer gave. It was just like Miss Dorothy and me again, back in Topeka! These dancers wore tights and knew a lot of stuff I did not know. We were whittled down to seven, then five and finally, there were four. I was one of them! *"Another opening, another show in Philly, Boston or Baltimore...."*

Paul, the show's choreographer, took me aside and remarked, "You don't know what you are doing, do you? You are a talented kid who needs ballet training. I will let you do the show but I want you to go to Ginger Burke's Royal Academy of Ballet on Hertle Avenue the day after the show closes!" I explained that I did not want to study ballet. I thought I would be better at jazz. I mentioned that I wanted to dance in Jerome Robbins' "West Side Story" in New York City. "Mr. Robbins won't give you the time of day without ballet training." I listened carefully.

After an amazingly enjoyable run with "Kate," I decided to go to Miss. Burke. Lessons were lessons. Perhaps she taught jazz, too. Time was marching on. I was in my senior year of high school and would be going to New York after graduation. I was going to become a professional dancer.

I began to get serious opposition concerning my career choice. I had not had opposition in the six years since my Father's death. Everyone loved the fact that I danced. They were proud of it. It seemed to add something to their lives. Now, it was Mother's grave concern that I would actually go to New York. It was the guidance counselors at high school who painted a future for me of low income, inferior life quality and exposure to the kinds of individuals one should basically steer clear of. In other words, I would make no money, eat hot dogs and be gay. They all brought up the subject of potential injury ruining such a career. I agreed to a meeting with Mother and the counselors. While explaining that I wanted to have a six month period to give myself a fighting chance in the "big city" with the "big guns" of the dance world, they were quietly holding their line. I had received a partial scholarship to a private high school earlier on. I was not able to accept that because we could not afford the balance of the tuition. Now a second scholarship opportunity, this time to college, came my way. They felt I should take it. I made it clear that college could wait. It was the type of meeting where no one party felt good about the outcome. I knew that I was disappointing them. They knew I was going to New York City.

Mother and I were close. I was the one in whom she confided. I was the offspring that would sit up late at night and listen to her. With me off to New York City, she would miss that interaction very much. I was sure that without my input, she might better find solace outside the home. As it happened, she began working soon after I left.

I needed to find a job that would provide me with more income so that I could save money for New York as well as help out at home. My current job at Howard Johnson's Ice Cream Store was not what I would need going forward. I began asking around for other opportunities. Very soon I learned that the manager of the Williamsville Inn in the nearby town of Williamsville, NY, was looking for a waiter. The Inn was an upper class establishment. The tips would be much larger there than at HoJo's (the local nickname for Howard Johnsons). Mr.

Moran, the Inn's manager, was welcoming to me. A big, burly type of man, he was as kind as he was stout. I would begin the following week, after giving notice to HoJos.

After working out schedules to coordinate between school, ballet lessons and work, I put the greater emphasis on the lessons. With one month of ballet classes behind me, I was smitten. I could not get enough of the technique, certainly not as fast as I would need it. Ginger was a darling of a woman who considered discipline the top priority, right up there with turned out legs! She was very interested in the work of George Balanchine, the Russian choreographer and director of the New York City Ballet, with whom she had connections. Two of her students were working with his organization, one in his School of American Ballet and one in the New York City Ballet Company.

One of the interesting things about Ginger was that her training was in Classical Ballet (Ballets Russes) but her focus was on the Neo-Classical, which she sensed was the new direction of ballet. Along with the others, I was the recipient of her very solid technical background. Her studio was comprised of professional as well as beginner students. Mickey DiFiglia, who later changed his name to Michael Bennett and became famous for creating the hit Broadway show "A Chorus Line," was then the most well known local dancer. All of us were her students, assigned to the appropriate class. I often observed the professionals in their class which took place after mine. I could then see what I needed to learn in order to be one of them. The gap was big.

Ginger also provided me with my first experience of seeing professional ballet on stage. It was the Bolshoi Ballet dancing *Walpurgis Nacht* at the O'Keefe Center in Toronto, Canada. The leading dancer was Maya Plisetskaya. Overpowered by what I was seeing, I was informed that this was the greatest ballet company in the world: an incomparable dancing troupe! Immediately after the performance, Ginger took us back stage. Some of us met the dancers in their dressing rooms. The men, removing their costumes, were chugging Vodka even before showering! They knew no English but were expected to sign autographs. Watching them fly around onstage and then seeing them as mere humans backstage, I was awakened to this art form and the human condition in the Soviet Union, all in one fell swoop. I have never forgotten that night. Now I had a realistic parameter. My career was going to be somewhere between "West Side Story" and the Bolshoi Ballet!

The plans for the Spring Break of Senior year were shaping up. My buddies, Andy and Jimmy, would join me for a trip to Manhattan. Andy was the world's next great musician, Jimmy was its next poet and I had a phone call to make to Jerome Robbins.

New York City

Our brief stay in Manhattan was everything each of us had hoped it would be, excepting that Jerome Robbins did not take my phone call. I did, however, see his Broadway production of "West Side Story." I was also taken back to my earlier yearning to dance jazz, back to that "Too Darn Hot" number and back to Dorothy Thompson's "Shuffle Off to Buffalo" routine. This was show biz! I also saw "Subways are for Sleeping," in which Michael Bennett was a chorus boy. I did not see a ballet.

I sensed that I could easily live in Manhattan. Furthermore, I could learn everything there. I was not overwhelmed by Manhattan. I saw it as a tool and still do. I had a reason for being there. It was the best place in the whole world to have a dance career, however, because there was more in that city than anyone ever needed, it didn't seem like the place to spend the rest of one's life. For that, Manhattan lacked everything one needed.

Back in Snyder, I focused on graduating, taking as many ballet lessons as I could squeeze in and preparing to leave my family. I was still butting the naysayers but things had quieted down, especially since my partner and I had won the Dance Championship of Buffalo in a televised competition that fall. We won with my version of the jitterbug against good competition from New York City.

On January 11, 1963, aboard a Greyhound Bus, I arrived in New York City. I had money and a place to stay. I had been told about the YMCA on West 27th Street and I had a job interview, courtesy of Mr. Moran, with a Mr. Grey at the Americana Hotel, 52nd Street and Broadway. It was enough.

The Americana Hotel was a fabulous place! Everywhere you looked was beautiful: Van Clef and Arpels diamonds, Gucci leathers, Valentino's designs, smoke shops, shoe shine vendors and bellhops in their wonderful-looking burgundy gabardine uniforms with matching caps! Working my way through the chandeliers and satin covered walls, I found Mr. Grey on the fourteenth floor. A cool approach compared to that of Moran, he managed to convince me that he was just thinking about me when I called up. The job opening was that of a room service waiter, 10pm to 7am five nights a week. The wage rate was ninety-five cents per hour. I could begin the following day. I took it.

    I phoned the School of American Ballet and learned that Balanchine's audition class was that afternoon at 4pm. I jotted down the address. The school was at 83rd St. and Broadway. The sunken, vast studios were accessed by a walk down a flight of stairs. Mr. Balanchine was impressive; so were his male students. Having taken my place at the ballet barre (structure on which dancers do their exercises), I felt the electricity in my heart and a lump in my throat. Mr. Balanchine did not look directly at me more than twice. I thought I did reasonably well in the class yet I did not get a response from him. After changing, I spoke with his secretary. She informed me that Mr. Balanchine felt I was insufficiently trained for my age. Ginger Burke had warned me of this when she insisted that I wait another six months before showing myself in New York City. However, the secretary said that Balanchine was interested enough to ask her make a call to Robert Joffrey. She smiled as she said this. She made it clear to me that this is not something Balanchine does often.

Robert Joffrey's American Ballet Center was the home of the Robert Joffrey Ballet. Its reputation was very good. Its history was only eight years long but its niche was made; the dance world looked upon the Joffrey enterprise as a major school and company. An appointment was made for me to take class at the Center. Mr. Joffrey would see me and seal my immediate future.

I left the Balanchine experience elated. I knew better than anyone that I had a slim chance at being accepted into a professional setting. But a chance I did have. After all I was male, good looking enough, tall and talented for dancing. Were I of the opposite sex, there would be no chance at all.

My new address was the Park Savoy Hotel, 58th Street and the Avenue of the Americas. Just six blocks from the Americana Hotel, my room came with maid service. I shared a bath with Myrtle who sold bras in the garment district downtown. The proximity of the hotels would prove to be very beneficial. I would be working throughout the night.

My audition class at the Joffrey School was taught by Rosa Sternov. She was a former star of the Metropolitan Opera Ballet. Her class was well within my powers. I liked her immediately, finding her to be glamorous but serious. The small, dark haired man watching the class was Robert Joffrey. His remarks to me after the class were very kind. He was clearly interested in having me be in his school. That interest extended to the offer of a full scholarship, provided I agreed to take four classes a day. He saw the deficiency in my training. He thought I could catch up.

Now I had a schedule: classes from 4pm-9pm, work from 10pm to 7am and sleep from 8am-3pm. I was elated. I couldn't wait to call home. I had left there four days earlier. As I dialed the number, I sensed that the reaction on the other end would not be nearly as elated. It wasn't. For Mother, the news meant that I would not be coming home. She also knew how happy I was. Our individual feelings were hard to disguise. She really did not have much to talk about with me. She warned me not to take money from strangers and to be careful of "those" people. She just did not know what else to say. I was a very reassuring son.

The only other person I knew in New York was Myrtle. We had agreed to have dinner together at the Flame Restaurant that night. It was my first day off after my first training day at the Americana. I had someone else to tell my good fortune to. When I walked into the Flame, I saw her sitting at a booth with her best friend, Alice. The two ladies made me feel that they were genuinely concerned about how I was doing and wanted to hear all about that. I remember our weekly dinners at the Flame for the comfort they gave to me. It was like having two Aunties who were rooting for you, right there across the street from Carnegie Hall!

I was also feeling that the job at the Americana would be a very good source of money. I didn't know that it would provide a favorite memory when a complaint to the room service manager about the waiter serving Ella Fitzgerald, America's greatest song stylist, put me into a new position of responsibility. Mr. Grey asked if I would address Ms. Fitzgerald's complaint. I was surprised that he would trust me to do that. He must have been testing me.

Ella Fitzgerald had just begun a two week gig at the Royal Box Ballroom in the Hotel. She did a ten o'clock show and a midnight show. It was her custom to have a hamburger and a Coca Cola in between shows. It was to be made accordingly: medium rare with raw onion, lettuce, no tomato but with lots of ketchup. She liked two lemon wedges in her coke. If possible, she wanted to have the same waiter each night. The first night's waiter had made mistakes in the order. I was pleased to see if I could provide this great entertainer with her requested meal.

After I knocked on her door, I heard the soft, oh so famous scatting. When the door opened, she stood there with a hanky in her hand and welcomed me into the room. I nervously awaited her verdict. A big smile came across her face. "I hope you will be able to come up every night with this order, young man. I don't have much time in between shows, so it is important that the order does not have to be sent back, you know?" I told her I would make arrangements to do that for her. She tipped me ten dollars. It meant coming in at 11pm on my two nights off but I was glad to oblige. By the third night of serving her, she asked that I stay awhile. She seemed to want someone to talk with.

Upon learning that I was studying dance, she exclaimed that she was a dancer before she was a singer. At the famous Apollo Theatre audition where she was discovered, Ella had prepared to dance for the audition. She had been the best block dancer in her home town of Newport News, Virginia. When she saw that the girls auditioning right before her were such very good dancers, she decided, on the spot, to sing instead. She recalled thinking how poorly she was received because the audience was so quiet one could "hear a pin drop!" Instead she won the competition hands down. Like future audiences would be the world over, that first audience was spellbound. She told me she always loved dancing first. She encouraged me to keep at it until it happened.

On the final night of her engagement, I asked her if I could somehow see her perform. I could not pay for it but I wouldn't have to be at a table as a member of the audience. She told me to come to the backstage area at 11:55pm. I was to ask for "Miss Ella." Her bodyguards would then know that she had arranged for me to come there. Standing only a few feet away from her, I listened: *Fly me to the moon, Oh the sharks have pearly teeth, dear, A tisket, a tasket, You'd be so easy to love....* We were all spellbound as Miss Ella took us on a journey to the stars and back! She was the real McCoy, certainly. You could "hear a pin drop!"

PROFESSIONAL TRAINING

Daily ballet classes, totaling twenty a week, initially shocked my muscular system; however, my imagination remained insatiated. Though my muscular structure was naturally tight, I was gaining elasticity. The natural shape of my legs resembled those of a trained dancer and my upper body projected way more than it knew. The combination tricked a lot of people into thinking I was a trained dancer.

Rosa Sternov was a consistently good teacher for the beginner student. Soon I was moved to David McClain's Intermediate class, alternating with Michael Lland's Intermediate Men's class. Completing my rosters of teachers was Lillian Moore who taught the Pirouette (turning) Class. McClain, looking every bit like a Madison Avenue executive, took a lot of interest in me. His was methodical and repetitive teaching. I developed well with him and was sorry that his departure for Columbus, Ohio occurred so early in my training. That left Lland, a former star of American Ballet Theatre (ABT) and a real poet of the stage. It was said that when he danced he resembled an archangel writing poetry in the air. His perfect fifth position belied any sense of poetry. He was all practical business in the class room. As I would improve a particular step in his class, he would caution me to "remember that for posterity, Robert!" I knew he could further develop my technique. At the very least he would impress me with the importance of that for ever more.

Miss Moore was first and foremost a ballet historian. Her several books on the subject were in their second and third printings. Everyone loved her Pirouette class. Who did not love to pirouette? Imagine a whole hour of it! She was to become my confidant. Her enthusiasm for my efforts seemed boundless. By year end Miss Moore had arranged for my first ballet performance: the Prince in the New Haven Ballet's production of "The

Nutcracker." She taught me the *grand pas de deux* (large step of two, commonly known as the main partnering between the leading dancers) and she also arranged for my costume. Then she proofed the photos of me in the costume. She was all about follow through. Examining the photos together, she would remark on what it was that I needed to work harder on in my classes. It was she I would later write to and it was she that gave one of those letters to the Library for the Performing Arts at Lincoln Center. It became a part of her archives and now my archives are also at the library.

By this time, I was fully acclimated to my weekly schedule. I knew this because I could tell that I wanted to find a girlfriend. Being one of the few straight boys in the school, it was my open playing field. Trinette was the beauty that I had been smitten with for some time. She entered the school at the same time I did. Her quality of the hometown girl in the big city was what attracted her to me. This quality belied the aristocratic features of her physical proportions. This dichotomy was fascinating. She was responsive to my approaches, easily accepting a date offer. We were both full scholarship students, having caught the eye of Joffrey, and had a definite future with the company. Trinette's dance attributes were of particular interest to Joffrey and he was very concentrated on her career. Her single mindedness paid off with a TIME MAGAZINE cover story on Joffrey's ballet "Astarte" in which she starred. The ballet world got her greater attention. I had to settle for her special "tomato pies"!

My need for finding a "deeper" relationship would be taken care of soon enough. Through a friend I learned of an apartment for sublet in Greenwich Village that belonged to Marnie, a dancer with the Merce Cunningham Modern Dance Company. That company was embarking on a six month tour of Europe and the Middle East. It was a way to start with my own place and leave the Park Savoy, Aunties and all. It would also mean looking for a different job in the Village. That would make things geographically sensible for a life so immersed in physical effort.

Marnie took me out to dinner to discuss the various responsibilities of subletting her place. This thirty-year old beauty from Portland, Oregon wanted to make sure that I would be able to manage the place and take care of the cat, *etc.* The evening ended in her bed and so ended my virginity. My "new" view of life was as spectacular as it has been for any male since the dawn of time. Marnie was a good lover, kind and caring. We had a week together before she left on tour; a perfect week for a first timer.

In the meantime, I also found Longchamps Restaurant. Located at 12th Street and Fifth Avenue, this quasi French bistro was a perfect next job in several ways. Location was ideal and hours were flexible; working most lunches and dinners only on the weekends. I was again sleeping when the rest of Manhattan was! It had been a long eight months of the previous schedule. I had a foot hold on the city and on what I was doing there. I knew that the training was the best available for me. I felt grateful to my teachers for their interest in my dancing but I began to sense that I needed to begin to get performance experience under my belt. I was trying to equate age with experience. To that end, I began to audition just for the experience of it. With the many professionals around, I had little chance of getting accepted yet.

Surprise! At the first audition Alicia Markova, the Metropolitan Opera Ballet director, selected me for a position with the Metropolitan Opera Ballet Company. The morning of the audition was memorable for the fact that a taxi ran over my feet at the corner of 39th St. and Broadway.

As I looked down at the tire mark on my shoes, I was amazed that I felt no pain. I went onto the audition, held by Markova herself. She had been a very great ballerina. I had heard of her pliant grace and porcelain quality. Attired in a black suit, heels and a pillbox hat, she took the class through its paces. I thought she looked wonderful as one of the principal dancers of the company lifted her overhead for her demonstration after class.

I had to tell the manager of the Met that I would get back to him about the contract. His puzzled look informed me that dancers don't usually respond to offers that way. I knew I couldn't accept the offer. It was too soon to take on a full-time dancing job. Again crossing Broadway to get the subway back to the Joffrey School, I carefully looked both ways and also down. The tire marks were still on my shoes. Maybe I was pushing my way into the profession just a little too fast.

I liked auditioning. I liked getting offers even better. I had to get a Broadway audition in before I could say I wouldn't ever dance there. Such a short time had passed since I wanted to do "West Side Story" and now I knew that I was only really interested in a ballet career. Ballet is that kind of experience.

The day after the Markova audition I found that I was going back to the Metropolitan Opera House; this time as one of Joffrey's guests for the opening night of the Royal Ballet's annual season. Margot Fonteyn, the great English ballerina, and Rudolph Nureyev, the famous Russian defector, were dancing the premiere of the ballet "La Bayadere." Though I had not seen either of them perform, I was taking classes with them at the Joffrey School prior to the opening night. During one class, Nureyev kicked the camera out of the hands of the Newsweek Magazine's photographer who had gotten too close to him, causing sudden concern and shock throughout the room. Though their new partnership was making a huge impact on the public, Nureyev was not yet accustomed to being famous. Margot Fonteyn was.

For the first time in my life, I fell in love. Fonteyn was everyone's favorite ballerina. I could see why. Her beautiful visual impact matched her artistic personality. The magical entrance she made in that ballet, crowned by the uniquely royal carriage of her torso, was the most captivating bit of theatre I had seen. In fact, I have not seen anything to equal that on the ballet stage since. Her overall impression was of such harmony and ease that I was convinced that I was only the latest person in this world to fall in love with her. Nureyev contrasted her like a wild panther to an English rose. His dancing was theatrical for its daring; so self absorbed was he in his work that when the white scarf of the pas de deux accidentally became entangled in Fonteyn's tiara, his eyes were anywhere but on her. As the audience gasped and the conductor slowed the orchestra to a grinding halt, Nureyev momentarily relinquished his absorbed manner long enough to help free her. Fonteyn went on to dance the full variation which came next in the ballet at the breakneck speed of a Balanchine dancer, getting every step in and on the music. The roar of the audience has not been equaled in my lifetime; a night to remember!

Within a week's time I had another big chance come my way. The new Bert Lahr musical "FOXY" was holding auditions. Here was a chance to do a Broadway audition and maybe meet the Lion from "The Wizard of Oz" at the same time. Again I was taken, offered a contract and this time I said yes because a Broadway show schedule would allow me to continue my full class schedule. Once the show was opened, one's whole day was free until show time. In a ballet company, on the contrary, one rehearses all day and dances at night as well.

Mr. Lahr observed the audition. We all got a chance to shake his hand and to listen to him speak for about ten minutes. The following day I phoned Longchamps to ask for an extended leave of absence but I did not call Joffrey. I sensed he would have tried to talk me out of the show.

Lahr was magical in the rehearsal room, staying clear of any famous "Oz" expressions that we were all looking for. One could learn from his work ethic: on time, economical and thoroughly professional. Of course his enthusiasm was contagious.

At the beginning of the third week of rehearsals, during a short break, Mr. Lahr suffered a massive coronary thrombosis. He died right there in front of us! The show was cancelled. The producers felt no other star could fit a vehicle created for Lahr. "FOXY" was not to be. This was the end of my Broadway pining. I returned to focusing on training and await my eventual fate: a contract with the new Joffrey Ballet.

It turned out that other gigs came up regularly. My next one was at the Caramoor Festival in Katonah, NY dancing a new ballet by choreographer John Butler. As it turned out, Virginia Williams, director of the Boston Ballet was watching the rehearsal one day with two of her dancers.

One of the dancers was Linda DiBona. Intent on working in the rehearsal, I was oblivious to the three of them sitting there. This would be the first and last time I would be unaware of being in a rehearsal room with Linda DiBona!

A Contract/Surprises

The reputed Joffrey Ballet Company suddenly was no more. After trying to appease his benefactor, Rebekah Harkness, Joffrey felt that he could not change the name of his company to the Harkness Ballet even if he would retain artistic directorship. The extremely wealthy Harkness was kind but unpredictable. She had long been a balletomane. Her first attempt at gaining control of her own company was similarly thwarted. At the time it was Jerome Robbins' Ballets USA that she supported. Robbins would have none of the "Ballet Benefactress Takes Over Company" scheme that it appeared Harkness was after.

That effort was not well known in the dance world. The Joffrey episode exploded on the front pages of all the newspapers.

Harkness ceased supporting the Joffrey Company, taking all but two of the dancers with her to form the Harkness Ballet Company. Throughout history there have been other benefactresses. Only those who put all their eggs in the one basket were vulnerable to an adverse outcome. Joffrey was feeling the pang of having doing so. Now he was broke with no other hand-outs and no board of directors. The entire dance community sided with him and looked to see how they could help him create another group of dancers, a new Joffrey Ballet. It was then that Trinette and I were among a handful of students in line for contracts to the new organization. The other dancers would be the two who stayed with Joffrey from the first company and professionals from other companies as well as one or two Broadway dancers.

While raising money and developing a Board of Directors, Joffrey began to have choreographers work with us. Initially these were experimental rehearsals. He brought in teachers from the Martha Graham Dance Company to work with us on modern floor technique and then choreographer Norman Walker came to ease that work into a contemporary ballet. Soon there was Lotte Goslar working with us on comedic movement and a strict ballet master from Madrid, Spain named Hector Zaraspe to act as ballet master. The in-house choreographer, Gerald Arpino, was also actively finding his way toward a new ballet with the new group.

Joffrey's signature eclecticism was apparent from the onset. He wanted to strike his own chord. He knew he could not compete with either the American Ballet Theatre or the New York City Ballet. He also knew he would now have to compete for dollars. We were the pawns with which this new venture would be played out. We all had the feeling, experienced and not, that this would be both a most exhilarating and a most exhausting period. Indeed, for the majority of us, it turned out to be both. Seven days a week, most weeks, and ten hours a day we toiled. The premiere of the company took place at Jacob's Pillow Dance Festival in Lee, Massachusetts in the summer of 1965. We danced Aprino's "Incubus" and "Viva Vivaldi" along with Walker's "Contrasts" and Goslar's "Charivari". "Incubus" was a dramatic work. "Charivari" was a ballet about clowns. The others were a classical and a contemporary ballet each.

Ted (Papa) Shawn, the co-founder of the "Pillow", welcomed us to his stage in a "barn", one on which many world famous dancers had performed. Performances were well received. We were very well rehearsed. There was a lot of excitement generated by the debut of the new Joffrey Ballet Company. It seemed everyone was rooting for us.

I remember not being able to sleep because the mosquitoes at the "Pillow" were so persistent. That along with the unusual heat made the week very restless. I whiled away the night hours after performances perfecting my high school Spanish with my Spanish speaking roommate, Luis. Zaraspe had brought Luis from Madrid. He was his prize pupil. He was now my prize English pupil as well.

And so the Joffrey Ballet was on the boards again and so were a number of us for the very first time. Though I was grateful for the opportunities afforded me, I thought I would never again feel really rested. Everyone had worked beyond their capacities. Everyone needed two weeks off. Before we were able to take that rest period we had one more week of performances.

Following the Pillow engagement, the company performed for a week at Central Park's Delacorte Theatre. This was the New York debut of the new company. The critics were kind. They wanted very much for the Joffrey Ballet to be fully resurrected. They also knew that it would take more doing to develop this company to the level of the former group. That group had taken eight years and many performances to shine as they did.

In the afternoon of the final performance, I retrieved the mail from my apartment. I opened a letter from the United States Department of Defense. It was a Draft notice. The escalation of the Vietnam War was proceeding in rapid order. Some of the other male dancers simply checked the "homosexual" box or the "conscientious objector" box on the form that was attached to the draft letters they had received. One was then immediately disqualified from serving his country. They couldn't have cared less. I thought about that for some time. I learned that the form became a permanent record. I cared about that. I would take the letter to Joffrey.

After the final curtain of the Delacort's performances, I received a knock on the dressing room door. A man handed me his card and asked if he could speak with me for a few minutes. WILFRED C. BAIN, DEAN of the SCHOOL of MUSIC, INDIANA UNIVERSITY, BLOOMINGTON, INDIANA, read the card. He complimented my performances with the company. He had seen three of the Park's performances. His dance department at the university needed a male dancer. If he offered me a full college scholarship in return, would I consider dancing at I.U.? College raising its head again, I must be imagining things! In surprising fashion, I said I would considerate it if I could study Political Science with Literature as a minor. He said I could major in whatever I wanted. Momentarily, I had forgotten about the draft notice. I took Dean Bain's offer and his card, telling him I would call him within a week's time. I needed to get to Joffrey.

The following morning I presented the draft notice to Joffrey. He told me not to worry about it. Attorney General Robert Kennedy had gotten a star of the New York City Ballet out of the draft. He would see to it that Kennedy got me out of it too. I thought I should tell him about Dean Bain at another time.

During our two week break I reconsidered checking one of the boxes. It would simplify things. Still, I could not convince myself to do it. I was experiencing "big picture" vision at the time. I was looking at the long range future. I chose not to question that. I had to count on Kennedy. Instead, I tried to envision the Army, envision not dancing. It was surprisingly easier to see myself not dancing. I had accomplished much in a short time. I was physically exhausted. The two years since I arrived in New York were packed with intense experiences. I had indeed learned a lot from living, working and training in the "Big Apple."

Joffrey's meeting with Kennedy had not been successful. At the end of September, I again received mail from the Department of Defense. It was an induction notice for October 20th. There was no other recourse left to me. I had "made my bed" so to speak. Joffrey and I had another meeting. I wanted him to know of my gratitude but also my feelings about my being pushed very hard. He needed us all to be more than we were. I understood that. Upon learning of the Indiana University offer and my acceptance of it, he all but gave up on my returning to the company. He asked me to teach my parts to my understudy, Don Richards. His disappointment was palpable. In the final days before my induction, I made a call to Indiana. Dean Bain told me he would hold the scholarship for me while I served my country. I was very surprised that he would do that. I thanked him. For the next two years I would not make a clear decision about what would happen after the Army. One needed to get through the Army, to avoid Vietnam!

My family was saddened by the news that I was drafted into the Army. As the middle son of a fatherless family, I was the son who would be selected. Murph was automatically eliminated because he was the eldest son of a fatherless family. Danny was physically unacceptable for military duty due to his history of polio.

I felt good about spending time at home with the family before the induction date. In the two years that I had been gone a lot of changes had occurred. The girls seemed grown up. Mother was despondent though still able to make an effort of good cheer now and then. The subject of the danger I would be facing was only slightly addressed during conversations. Murph felt the impact but said little. There wasn't a lot to say. Our interests were so different that I think we had developed a real admiration for each other. I know I was very proud of his sports skills. It was always wonderful to watch him play basketball; he seemed to dance on the court, so natural were his athletic movements!

I took on my part as a comforting son and interested brother. I spoke of the periods of time that I could come home on leave. I would write often. Still, the feeling that I was about to be EXECUTED permeated the atmosphere at home.

A Grateful Soldier

Embarking on a two year hiatus was one thing, experiencing the United State Army was another. The only aspect of military life I would relate to would be the discipline and sense of order required of new recruits. Ballet dancers know about those attributes.

Having an M-16 rifle in my arms was a long way from rehearsing ballets in the Joffrey Company. The next eight weeks of Basic Training would be a lesson in contrasts from what I had spent the last two years doing. One thing was clear from the onset: I would have little time to think about anything but learning how to be an effective soldier.

    We arrived at Ft. Dix, New Jersey by train. The average age of the recruits was nineteen. The average education level was mid- high school. These were gas pumpers, gofers, landscapers, dropouts and a ballet dancer. These were mostly undereducated young men for whom the military would be something more than a stepping stone. The rest of us were caught in the middle of a conflict that was drawing more protesters as it was escalating. Early on I decided to conform. I wanted to gain something from the time I would spend in the military. If I could learn about things that would be valuable to me later in life, I could then feel that I took something away with me when I was discharged. It would be a way to make greater sense of having "lost" two valuable years. This approach would prove rewarding in several ways; the results would be gains not losses.

    Immediately I was struck by the thoroughness of the training. If one paid attention, one could survive a war experience. The goal was to make the soldier so prepared that he could not only save himself but others as well. The key ingredient was discipline. It made perfect sense.

    My attitude was noticed. Upon arrival at my first command post in Ft. Bragg, North Carolina, I was promoted. I had arrived at Ft. Bragg after six weeks of advanced individual training in Chemical Equipment Repair at Ft. McCallum, Alabama. I was trained to repair gas masks and flame throwers. I began to look into the offer to begin a college education while in the Service. Perhaps I could get English 101 and 102 completed in the night classes.

Ft. Bragg was home for thirteen months. One could settle in. One could also get to know the men one would live with; twenty five people in one barracks, ten barracks to a platoon. My promotion enabled me to earn the position of Barracks Leader. It meant, among other things, that I ran the daily cadence exercises and oversaw the condition of the soldier's spaces (footlockers, *etc.*) for the purpose of random inspections. All that talk about perfectly rolled socks and underwear had an ultimately positive effect on the average psyche. This provided further confirmation of the many good results that "structure" offered young people. My position also gave me the opportunity to get on the trusting side of the men I oversaw. I was the one, after all, of whom they were suspect. It was MY manner that they watched closely. A ballet dancer was something they knew nothing about. This was the Motorcycle/Motown crowd!

Speaking with them, answering their questions and asking what their lives were like before being drafted, I gained their trust and confidence. It was unusual for us to have time to talk leisurely. We managed to get to know one another while spit shining boots and cleaning M-16 rifles.

Their interest peaked; one of them brought me a news article about the Joffrey Ballet's upcoming performances at Chapel Hill, North Carolina. Would I take them to see a performance? Surprised by the question, I took it seriously. I asked for a list of interested names.

On a Saturday evening, seven of us traveled by bus to see the performance. It had been six months since I was drafted. I had written my share of letters to family and friends, colleagues in the ballet and, of course, to Miss Moore. Trinette knew that I was coming to the performance. I thought about her a lot. I wanted to see her again.

We arrived an hour before curtain time. Tickets in hand, I opted out of going to dinner with the troops. This was a chance for me to spend time with my ballet friends backstage. I told the troops that I would meet them at the seats ten minutes before curtain time and that I would take them backstage after the show.

Before I saw Trinette, Joffrey saw me. He was anxious about one of the dancers who had sprained an ankle in the afternoon rehearsal and could not dance in the opening ballet, Aprino's "Olympics." Would I do him a big favor? Would I dance the part in "Olympics" that I was learning when I left the company? I thought he was pulling my leg. If he was, it was one hell of a way to greet me.

Trinette tapped me on the shoulder. I thought perhaps she told Joffrey that I would be coming to the show. He seemed so ready to see me. I paused to look at them both and realized that he was not pulling my leg. I had to help out. I asked if we could have a run-through onstage after I warmed up. He called to Aprino to find me the costume, shoes etc. My head started to spin. Was this happening? Trinette was thrilled that I said yes. I did not even give the troops a second thought.

With the other 'athletes' onstage giving me their words of encouragement, we began the rehearsal. I spent the most time on the sections of the ballets where we were all onstage together. The solo work I would remember as best I could, but I could not improvise the group work. At the ten minute call, I thought of the troops taking their seats in the theatre. I could only laugh at the preposterousness of it all. They would never believe that I did not set this up! With the torch bearer circling the stage, the curtain rose on "Olympics." I could hear mumbling in the audience. It had to be the troops!

I felt like I was on a very rough ride, though considering everything, the performance came off well. The work stood on its own merits. After cleaning up and getting dressed, I met the troops at their seats for the beginning of the third ballet of the evening. "High Fives" and raised eyebrows were evident everywhere. They whispered, "Brassel that was very cool. We thought you might be up to something. You GOTTA teach us that when we get back to the barracks!" They wouldn't believe the real story.

After the show, I took them backstage. They seemed mesmerized. Though some of the dancers did not quite know how to react to their visitors, understandably, their visitors knew that they had just witnessed something they had never seen before. They were not about to forget it. Back at the barracks, on glassy terrazzo flooring, these guys in socked feet were attempting the steps they saw onstage. They carried on until two in the morning. I have often thought of that night and the opportunities it offered all of us. I have also often wondered if they ever saw a ballet again. I know it was an unforgettable experience for them. I sensed that my muscles would not let me forget the experience the following morning.

The Commanding Officer (CO), whose gofer I had become (complete with jeep!) handed me a note the following morning. A local ballet teacher was requesting that I start a boy's class at her school. It appears that she read an article in DANCE MAGAZINE that I was stationed at Ft. Bragg. I had begun giving private lessons to the daughters of some of the Officers. One of them was a student of the local teacher. I jumped at the thought of working with young boys in dance. Though I was not a teacher, I thought I could help them with the manner in which they carried themselves and used their arms. Such aspects of male dancing made the difference. Any dancer could teach steps.

To my great surprise, I found thirteen nine and ten year

olds in the class. They were well prepared for me, standing there in their white T-shirts, black tights, white shoes and socks; the Joffrey apprentice uniform! Though I had them for only a few months, I got a very good idea of what I could do one day as a teacher of ballet. Suddenly, my time with them was cut short.

Orders from Washington arrived. Our company, the 16th Light Equipment Maintenance Co. (General Support) was ordered to spend a thirteen month tour of duty in Danang, Vietnam. I had only nine months left before I would be out of the Army! I wasn't going to avoid Vietnam after all. Immediately the two hundred and fifty platoon members were sent six miles north of Ft. Bragg to "Vietnam Village." There the military had set up a replica of a Vietnamese village, complete with the local Asians playing the role of the Vietcong. Again, I was impressed with the training. Through the actual firing of rubber rounds at us while we used crawling techniques that kept the hips to the ground, the training was intended to keep us alive. At any hour of the night, while sleeping in the foxhole wearing full gear, the sergeants would call out "War." Our technique would be scrutinized and bodies would be tagged DEAD if the performance fell short. The intensity wasn't so different from a stage performance with the exception that dancers don't eat out of metal dishes and drink out of canteens while freezing outside in what felt like the dead of winter.

On January 11, 1967 at 7pm the full platoon reported to the Ft. Bragg airfield. Our underwear had been dyed green and our home leaves were taken. Our flight, scheduled for 9pm, would take us to Oakland, California where we would board a Navy ship for the voyage to Danang, Vietnam. Even though we were so well prepared, none of us could believe that we were actually going. Thoughts of that EXECUTION atmosphere back home entered my head.

When at midnight we were still awaiting the flight to Oakland, the CO called Headquarters in Washington, DC. The flight had taken off, and on time, from FT. BELVOIRE, WASHINGTON! On board was the 16th Light Equipment Maintenance Co. (Direct Support). The Direct Support Company was the company required in Danang. We would NOT be going to Vietnam! The confusion from the very beginning was the similarity in the names of the two companies. The CO announced the news using the airfield's loudspeaker. I foresaw a choreographic event about to happen. On the tarmac were all the troops, their wives, children and friends. It suddenly looked like an Arpino ballet. They were jumping, rolling on one another and swinging their loved ones in circles. Suddenly, none of us could believe we were NOT going. It really did feel like it was too good to be true. Three weeks later new, different orders were delivered. This time we got on that plane and on that Navy ship. This time we landed on the island of Okinawa.

I had six months left in the Army!

Situated on the East China Sea, this Ryukyu Island was populated with US military personnel, Quonset Huts, Steam Bath/Massage Parlors and smiling Asian faces. The military's first line of defense was Sex; how to take care of oneself in downtown Naha. The Asian women had been reared to satisfy their male counterparts. This extended to doing the hard labor of the work force as well as take care of any and all other needs.

Our purpose on Okinawa was exactly what our general support company was trained for; my job was to manage the requisitioning of parts from Washington that would be used to salvage the war-torn gas masks and flame throwers. In an airport hanger sat my charges: 750 local assembly men and women as well as a troop staff of twenty. Once the orders were made for the day, I was basically free. The system was in place before we arrived. We were replacing the troops who had been there for thirteen months and had just returned to the States. With this type of setup, who would not enjoy these last six months?

During the third week on the island, I was asked to deliver a package to the choreographer of the USO shows. When we met, he looked carefully at my nametag. "Brassel, I saw you dance at the Delcorte Theatre in Central Park!" He was unaware that I had been drafted but he was very happy to see me there. He knew someone else who would be happy too.

Her name was Irmgard. She was a former Kirov ballerina

who had married a US Army First Sergeant. Her future husband, Ted, had been stationed in Stockholm. During a visit to Leningrad, they met and fell in love. At the time I arrived on the island, Irmgard was operating a ballet school. The choreographer could not wait to introduce us.

The next afternoon he set up a time when we could all meet. It was then that I learned the ballet studio was a stone's throw away from my Quonset hut. We decided to meet at the studio. The studio was in Irmgard's home; an elaborated hut. The family, including Irmgard's husband Ted, their ten year old daughter Diana and the two dogs, was there for the introduction. One would have easily thought that Prince Charming had arrived on Okinawa. Indeed, it was the first time Irmgard had met a professional male ballet dancer in uniform.

The family was lovely and very kind. Irmgard was beautiful. It was decided that evening that I should use the studio to get back into shape. How very fortunate for me. I could not have imagined a better arrangement now that I was officially a "short timer." That used to be the talk in the early days of basic training. One could not wait until they had less than six months to go before they would be out of the service. Then they were considered a "short timer." Only then would they begin checking off the days until freedom.

It began simply enough. The first time Irmgard and I were alone together was in a ballet class.; she teaching me in her studio. We planned to meet each day at approximately the same time. Eventually she joined me at the ballet barre. Though it had been fifteen years since she performed, she looked very good. Her training was still evident. I was very unsure of whether I would get into the condition I remembered. What I saw in the mirror was different from what I wanted to see. I was quite weak on my legs, more so than I expected to be.

Gradually the strength came, slowly I felt better about my technique. I was quite grateful to Irmgard for her encouragement, her corrections, for her being there. I found myself spending more time with her. I liked Ted very much. When he was around, he was very interesting. He talked about all things European. I liked listening to him. Eventually, I began to sleep over. Irmgard and I would take Diana and the dogs to the sea on the weekends while Ted worked or slept. He often did not feel well.

As a twenty-two year old, I found myself physically attracted to Irmgard. Being a forty year old woman, she was responsive to my vibrations. The more time we spent together the more we learned about one another. I was also keen on learning more about the island and its people. Unlike the other GIs who were spending a lot of their "off" time in downtown Naha at the "district," I was being shown the island's beauty and learning about the native customs from one who had been there for ten years and was eager to introduce me to all of it.

Time was getting very short. I was a much stronger dancer. We filmed a pas *de deux* that I choreographed. It was to be a part of a larger project for the Ryukyu Islands Arts Education Program for the Middle School system. It would represent the arts of Music, Painting, Opera and Dance. Unfortunately, I did not get to see the finished product before I left Okinawa.

That nearly did not happen as scheduled because the six-day Israeli war broke out two weeks before I was to leave. All Discharge orders were put on temporary hold. As my luck would have it, the War ended and I left as scheduled. Our goodbye was hopeful. I felt I would see her again at some point in the future.

Nine hours into the flight to Oakland Air Base, a huge white light overtook the World Airlines 747 aircraft. If one was not awake at the time, he was awakened. I thought about the International Dateline, wondering if the light was the Dateline. It was something that I had heard occurs over that part of the Pacific Ocean. The plane began to descend. The stewardesses started handing out ear plugs. The weight of the plane seemed to suddenly lighten. The ears plugs did not help very much; we dropped too fast. Over the loud speaker the pilot described our mysterious descent and explained that by opening the belly of the plane to release the cargo into the ocean, he was able to measurably slow the descent. He asked the eight individuals sitting next to the shoot releases to identify the handles. He was preparing us to slide into the water before the plane did.

Everyone already had life preservers tied on except eighty-four year old Martha, a cripple, who was sitting on my left. She had visited the island to be with her son and his family. She was on her first-ever flight, having crossed the Pacific on a ship to get there. She insisted that I wear two preservers so I would be sure to survive. "You are so much younger than me," she said. On my right was Patrick who was returning from the front lines of Vietnam. He was one of the eight to get his hand on the shoot handle. He was also crying hysterically, shouting that for thirteen months he had survived "Nam" and now he was going to go like this. Within seconds he pulled the handle before further instruction. The ceiling of the aircraft directly over us began to open, slowly, in a hydraulic manner.

Blankets and pillows were sucked into the opening. I grabbed the handle and, with the advice of a stewardess, pushed in the opposite direction, my hand on top of his. The aircraft was now obviously leaning very much to the left, we on the right side of the aisle looking down on those on the left side of the aisle. We flew tilted like this for the remainder of the flight. One could feel the plane no longer descending.

A sudden jerk and a thrust forward were the final fearful sounds the airplane made before touching down on the tarmac in Anchorage, Alaska. As we deplaned, we were met by ambulances, fire trucks and police cars. Entering the airport, the Eskimos placed paper hats rimmed in fake fur around our heads; their welcoming gesture was somehow greater than our harrowing ordeal. Martha instructed me to get her to the nearest Delta Airline counter as soon as possible. She was intent on getting home to Toledo, Ohio as soon as she could.

The captain had other plans for all of us. We were to go into a large debriefing area. Martha would have none of it. That was for military personnel only, she said. Though this would be only her second flight, she was not afraid to get onto another airplane. She was as determined as she had been about that life preserver. I obliged her command. There was a flight departing for Toledo. I stayed with her all the way to the tarmac. The stewardess took her from there. She asked me to lean down to her wheelchair. She kissed my cheek saying, "I have had a very good life, now it is your turn Robert. God Bless!"

During the three days we were detained in Anchorage we learned, among other things, that the far engine on the right wing had exploded causing the aircraft to react as it did. Our good fortune was the pilot's expertise in decision making and his final hour of handling that aircraft.

My military career had come to a safe conclusion. I was free to go home to Buffalo. I dwelled for some time on the entire experience. A keen sense of gratitude overcame my thoughts. I had grown up. I was content about my circumstances. I had learned about people and places that enriched my sense of the world. I was content that I had served my country and knew that, were I to have to make the choice again, I would do it again. There was also a strong sense that something was captured that could never be captured at a different time in this life. I had become a man.

My Way Back

Twenty-five thousand students swarmed Indiana University's vast campus. The campus was surrounded by Fraternity and Sorority Houses, an occasional shopping plaza and an abundance of ice cream parlors. The campus took up the entire town of Bloomington. Clearly, this was not only a seat of higher learning but of higher partying as well.

The School of Music was renowned in the professional world for its Opera department. Many alumni had gone on to have celebrated careers. Dean Bain was intent on making as much of the dance department. Having hired Gilbert and Nancy Reed, former dancers from American Ballet Theatre, to head the department, he felt he was on the right track.

After signing in for my academic classes, I met with the Reeds. I liked them immediately. Their solid backgrounds were evident in our initial meeting. Given the unfamiliar atmosphere I was in, I found that comforting. They informed me that I was the only male dancer at I.U. and would be busy with rehearsals and performances for the winter season. Gilbert had four ballets planned.

Later that evening, back at the apartment that I shared with a biology student, I looked over my schedule. Eighteen credit hours that included English 103, World History, Political Science, Intro to Literature and a Math course would have to fit in and around the ballet schedule. I thought it might not be possible. I already had placed my priorities on the academic schedule but I knew the requirements of ballet. I decided to request that Dean Bain find at least one other male dancer to join the dance department.

Everything began at once. It was a challenge for me to get used to being in school fulltime. I was up until two in the morning doing homework. It was a pleasure to work with the Reeds. The girls I worked with in the dance department were also of high caliber. The only missing element here was more men. Dean Bain did not come up with another male dancer for the department.

As the semester moved onward, I was getting thinner. My energy level was very high. The combination was enough to spell trouble. No one was addressing the way I seemed to be "disappearing". My energy fooled all of us until one day I decided to go to the doctor for a check up. I had not been able to shake a cold. "Well, young man, you have the flu! But you also have a large lump on you neck. How long have you had that?" he asked.

I hadn't noticed the lump. He asked me to have an x-ray done. This, happening the week of the performances and at the end of the semester during mid- term examinations, would shed a whole new light on my short college career. I had the x-ray done and returned to rehearsals.

At the post performance party, with Alicia Markova and Robert Joffrey in attendance, I was speaking with Joffrey when I involuntarily dropped the glass of juice I was holding onto the floor. I could not feel my hand holding it. Joffrey said he thought I danced well but that I was obviously overworked. He and Markova had flown in for the performances to see the Reed ballets with the chance that they might want one of them for their respective repertoires.

I was very ill. The x-ray revealed a growth on the thyroid gland; the diagnosis was hyperthyroidism. I was asked to decide on an operation to remove the growth or medication for the rest of my life. Fortunately, I had a four week break before the beginning of second semester. I took the medical reports home to Buffalo with me, telling the university doctor that I would let him know of my decision.

The day before my surgery at Buffalo General Hospital, my midterm examinations marks arrived: a 3.3 class average. I was happy about that though I had already sensed that it would be the last marks I would be awaiting. My college career was over. I took little time during the pre- surgery period to remind myself that the dance career could not wait. I had always been right about that. I had been always a dancer! Certainly I would not want to spend any of my better years dancing at a university. I needed to get back into the big pond. First, I needed to get healthy.

Two months after the surgery I was settled with a pill a day to balance my thyroid reading; the results of a less than successful surgery. I felt very well, well enough to arrange for my return with to the Joffrey Ballet. Suddenly, another severe setback occurred that would delay that return.

I had developed a case of pleurisy. It was to be the final resolution to months of being overworked and overextended. The doctors were only somewhat successful in extracting the fluid from my lungs. The fluoroscope detected residual fluid. Seriously considering my career choice, the doctors told me it was unlikely that I would dance again. I would not be able to get enough oxygen into my lungs at one time nor would I be able to bend the left side of my back without pain.

For the first time, I decided to trust my body to let me use it fully. I would not only take the medical advice. I also called Ginger Burke, my first ballet teacher, to ask what time the beginner adult/teen class was scheduled for. She knew my situation and was awaiting my call. I planned on working slowly. After the first class, Ginger and I went to see the Merce Cunningham Company's performance at Baird Hall, the same hall where I did "Kiss Me Kate." It would be interesting to see the company which I had only peripheral attachments to. Though Marnie had retired, our mutual friend Sandra was still with the group.

Ginger and I went backstage to say hello to Sandra. Hugging me a little more than casually she said, "Bob, Don Richards stepped onto a land mine in Vietnam on Christmas day. His legs were blown off. He died the following day!" I turned away and began to weep. Don was my understudy at the Joffrey Ballet. Upon my departure for the Army, Don received a contract from Joffrey to replace me. Within months he, too, was drafted. I felt cold with the realization. I decided there and then that when I got back to performing, I would also perform for Don. Indeed, his smiling face came to mind many times before I made future stage entrances.

My body got better. Continuous, slow, musical movement

became my medicine. I found that within a month, I was doing the advanced class at Ginger's. The doctors did not think I was actually able to do what I told them I was doing. I decided not to have another fluoroscope test, as recommended. I was afraid of the results. Instead, I made plans to return to New York. I would leave the following week. It was March 1, 1968.

A two year hiatus, four grueling months of overextending one's physical capacity at college and three months of illness recovery are a lot for this "miracle" that we walk around in. I found comfort knowing that I had a basically strong constitution.

Upon returning to the Joffrey, I was greeted with warmth and kindness. This was my professional family, so to speak. I was also painfully aware that I reminded them about Don. He was the "son" who would not be returning. Everything had changed; many new dancers and many new ballets. Trinette looked wonderful. A new work for her was making sensational news: Ballet's first rock ballet, "Astarte.. This was a big push for what was now called the City Center Joffrey Ballet. The spring season was just about to begin. I began taking classes and looking for a waiter's job while I got back in shape.

L'Orangerie French restaurant on East 53rd St. and Lexington Avenue had an opening for a waiter- in- training. The level of service would require skill. I was learning how to place ice cubes into glasses with serving spoons, flambé entrees at tableside, bone fish and remove lobster tail all while keeping a white, long napkin over my forearm. Choreography like this I never imagined! However, I had been around the block with food service. At this point in time I needed a lot of money for few hours. I needed the best of what the city had to offer a waiter. I found it at L' Orangerie. The tips averaged $50 per table. One could make $150-200 having merely three tables at the dinner seating. I would not need to work every dinner of the week. What I needed was to get back on the dance track.

The "rooms for rent" ad promised a one- room with shared bath for the right price. The address was on West 71st St. and Central Park West. I took it. Set to work, I was back where I belonged and all would again be right with the world.

All was not right with the City Center Joffrey Ballet, however. I did not like what I saw on the stage. There was more main stream concept and less classical dancing. I was suspect. Joffrey, being such a classicist, was selling out. For me, this was a dilemma. I saw several evenings of performances before I decided that I did not want to rejoin the company.

I was taking daily classes at the Joffrey School. It was thought that I would be rejoining the company after the six week spring season. I was very unsure of my retraining and less sure of where I would end up but I knew I wanted to get to know the people at American Ballet Theatre. It was a dream of a repertoire at ABT. The dancers were very established. The company had stars. I would not be able to judge how well I would be received until I took a subway ride over there.

After the season, I asked to have a meeting with Joffrey. I expressed my change of heart about the type of ballets I wanted to dance. I thought that, with enough work, I could dance the princely roles of classical ballet. I wanted to dance "Swan Lake," "Giselle," and "The Sleeping Beauty," the roles of Siegfried, Albrecht, and Florimund. We both knew it was a long shot. Still, it was within the realm of possibility. I had the stature. I also had enormous competition. Joffrey was disappointed in the way that a father might be in his son. He had trained me and hoped that I would be successful with and for him. He indicated that there was an act of dishonor in my decision. I understood that.

The following week I met with Leon Danielian, Director of the ABT School. I had been taking classes with him and he wanted me to join ABT. The company had just departed for a tour of Japan and, when they returned, he thought it would be exactly the right time for me to audition for Lucia Chase, the director of ABT. I continued taking classes at the school with Leon Danielian and Valentina Pereyaslavec while continuing at L'Orangerie.

Danielian surprised me with an interim tour possibility dancing with the Garden State Ballet (GSB), located in Newark, New Jersey while I was waiting for ABT to return from Japan. The time frame fit perfectly. The GSB was embarking on a six week tour of the state of New Jersey. ABT would be returning to New York just as GSB was ending its tour. He called Fred Danieli (formerly of New York City Ballet) who co-directed GSB and made the contact. The audition was scheduled for the following day. This could signal the end of my starring role at L'Orangerie!

The Danielis (wife Evelyn was the company's business manager) were very welcoming. I had a very good referral. I hoped that I was what they needed. The class was given by James Clouser, a choreographer. It was great fun, but it was hardly an orthodox ballet class. Like most choreographers teaching a class, including Mr. Balanchine, Clouser was more interested in movement and how it worked than in properly teaching a ballet class. His class was probably a good idea for an audition. The director could watch me try out some of the actual choreography that was in the tour's ballets. It is also an easier audition than the normal class structure where any and all of one's faults are exposed.

After the class Fred took me into his office to sign a tour contract. As I was signing the contract, he asked if I could stay and watch a rehearsal in studio "A".

He wanted me to keep my eye on the ballerina working on the ballet "Symphony in C." My life was about to be changed forever.

Falling in Love Again, For Real

As my dance bag slid off my shoulder, I leaned against the ballet barre gazing in awe. Here was the match for Fonteyn, only somewhat smaller. Here was some intent, some proportion, and some dark haired beauty! When I first saw her, she was in a *presage* (overhead lift) position of 1st *arabesque* (legs making a right angle). Her steady partner slowly lowered her to the floor where, in quicksilver fashion, she repeated the line *a terre* (on the floor).

Clapping hands always stopped a rehearsal. Fred called a

five minute break, taking me around to meet several of the dancers. As we got to Linda DiBona, he asked if I could try a few things with her. The partner showed the steps and then I tried them with her. The first one worked fine; *soutenou en de dans to pique arabesque (*an inside turn ending on one leg while the other leg in lifted behind*)*. We tried it again. We went on to a promenade which ended in a lunge. It also worked fine. I really wanted to try that again but she was intent about going on to the next part. An arrow had struck through my heart back at the *barre*. I was in love with her! I soon learned that everyone loved her. She was, at once, wonderful and mysterious. Small talk was cut by the clap of the hands. They would run through the second movement once more before calling it a day. I was left spellbound by the way she worked; an experienced dancer, one could see her working her way into the choreography using the music totally. I imagined her onstage. Wow!

    She left the studio directly, as though she had another rehearsal to get to. I walked out with Fred who asked me to learn the ballet. Of course she was no where to be found once I had changed and was ready to get the bus back to New York. Evelyn stuck her head out of the office, the same as she did into the rehearsal twenty minutes earlier. "Linda takes the bus back to New York also!" Was she reading my heart's mind? I smiled and inquired what time Linda rehearsed the following day. Smiling back, Evelyn directed me to the call board.

Putting my fare into the collection machine, I turned to the left to look for a seat. Linda was sitting about a third of the way back, next to the window. Though there were many empty seats on the bus, I asked her if I could sit with her. As she nodded she turned her beautiful head toward the window. I noticed the off-white silk blouse with the matching covered buttons. It was so right on her. The whole package was world class!

After several one word answers to my first questions, she told me that she lived on the upper west side. She had three roommates and a cat that had just had kittens. The trip passed timely, ending with my remarking on how we had found each other, there on the bus. She did not respond. Sometime later while on tour, we spoke of past experiences and of the first time she had come to New York City. She danced at Hunter College with the Boston Ballet. The following day she, another dancer and her ballet director from Boston watched a rehearsal of John Butler's ballet which was being prepared for the Caramoor Festival in Katonah, NY. That was my rehearsal with John Butler four years earlier when I totally missed seeing her for the first time. Having 'found' her on the bus, I felt the hand of Fate these four years later. It all made perfect sense to me!

I offered to see her to her apartment but when she learned that we took difference subways home, she declined. I knew I would take her home the next time. We were going to be working together for six weeks. As we parted, my feet were barely touching the pavement. I felt like I had found the girl of my dreams that day, a girl so unlike any other, a girl who I must have been destined for. Here was a real dream of a girl!

The tour began in Red Bank, New Jersey. Each town and city was prefaced by a new rehearsal and cast changes. Apart from being onstage again and learning new works while waiting for my "big" opportunity with ABT, this tour, for me, was about Linda DiBona, the girl and the ballerina. Like others before me, I was captivated by her performance quality; here was containment and joy, classical carriage with a sense of abandonment, solid technique that gave the impression that she was not even aware she was in pointe shoes. That, I thought, was how pointe dancing should be. That, I remembered, was the Fonteyn quality. Watching Linda work and perform on a daily basis was a lesson in and of itself.

In time I was able to be with her alone; a cup of coffee here, a sandwich there. I began to learn about her background, training and how she considered the repeated Fonteyn comparisons. I learned that she was twenty-two and, at that age, the comparisons to the great ballerina were very flattering. She had nothing more to say about that. The lack of excess in her dancing was represented in her offstage personality. This was the quality everyone loved about her. It enhanced the mystery. The more I got to know her, the more I realized just what a prize she was!

Of course word spread throughout the company that I was "falling" for her. It must have been quite obvious. I was trying to figure out a way to be alone with her before asking if I could come to her room. The stage manager saved the day by letting me use his car on a company day off. We had a wonderful time in Vineland, New Jersey traveling through the countryside, having a lunch outside in the brisk November air all the while both realizing what we really wanted to be doing by the end of the day. We arrived back at the hotel to watch the returns of the presidential election. Once Nixon was declared the winner, I made my move. The following morning was my twenty-fourth birthday!

As the tour ended, the great dancing movie star Gene Kelly came from Los Angeles to be the Master of Ceremonies for the GSB fundraising Gala Performance in Newark, New Jersey. This master of the dance, though retired by that time, exuded charm and smoothness, even at the microphone. He told Hollywood stories and showed a film clip from "Singing in the Rain." His presence was certainly an inspiration to all of us.

It was the tour's final performance. As was fitting, someone had placed one red rose and a box of chocolates on our bed in the hotel room that night: a tour to remember, a director's wife to thank and a ballerina for me to someday marry!

Though it would be a long time before our relationship could be developed, it was clear that we were in love with each other. Following the tour with GSB, we went separate ways professionally. Linda joined the Harkness Ballet of New York and I joined ABT. It was the beginning of our jumping hurdles just to be in the same place together; the start of a long, often separated relationship.

Within weeks, Linda began a six month tour of Europe while I remained in New York rehearsing for a nine week tour of the United States. I felt the threat of her absence. Someone could easily come between us in that length of time. I had to put it out of my mind. Fortunately I had the whole of ABT to grab my attention; the stars, the ballets, the teachers, ballet masters and the thought of revisiting some of the cities of my youth. I intended to write a lot of letters to Europe. It was the only way to keep myself in her mind while we danced the time away until we could again be together.

American Ballet Theatre, our country's greatest exponent of the ballet art, was a company on the run. Without the government sponsorship that major foreign companies enjoyed, ABT was to America what the Royal Ballet was to England and what the Bolshoi Ballet was to Russia. ABT's main benefactress was also it artistic director, Lucia Chase. Since 1940 it has brought ballet performances to the hinterlands as well as the larger cities. Its reputation for theatre ballets and stars was unequalled in our country. Being accepted into this organization was akin to learning all there was to learn about dance; a PhD. of ballet.

Lupe Serrano, Royes Fernandez, Johnny Kriza, Ruth Ann Koesun, Sallie Wilson, Scott Douglas, Toni Lander, Eliot Feld, Cynthia Gregory, the lists of stars went on and on. On the horizon for the coming season would be the first glimpse of the celebrated partnership of Italy's Carla Fracci and Denmark's Erik Bruhn. The ballets were no less stellar than their creators: Anthony Tudor's "Lilac Garden," "Pillar of Fire" and "Dark Elegies," Jerome Robbins' "Fancy Free," "Les Noces" and "Interplay," George Balanchine's "Theme and Variations," Agnes DeMille's, "Fall River Legend," "Rodeo" and "Three Virgins and the Devil" were all performed along with new works by Eliot Feld, Michael Smuin, Dennis Nahat and Alvin Ailey. Surrounding all these works were the masterpieces of the Romantic and Classical eras: "Les Sylphides," "Giselle," "Romeo and Juliet," "La Sylphide," "Coppelia" and "Swan Lake." All of these magnificent dancers, choreographers and productions were developed under the steady gaze of Lucia Chase.

I was humbled and excited at being selected to join this lofty company but I was more excited to get on with the rehearsals and to get to know the ballets and the people surrounding them.

Loftiness aside, the work began in a run down studio on the east side of town, impossible to get to and without bathrooms. We used those in the restaurant next door. Leonide

Massine took the first rehearsal for his ballet, "Gaite Parisenne." This historical figure, then eighty-three years old, was one of the stars of the film "The Red Shoes." He had worked with Diaghilev's Ballet Russes and was still rehearsing his works around the world.

I remember him coming into the studio, just as company class was ending. He approached me to ask if I would take care of his watch while he rehearsed. I put his timepiece on my wrist and I watched him rehearse his ballet for what was to be the last time. He took ill during our rehearsal period and his daughter, Tatiana, came on tour to continue working with us. His spirit for that particular ballet was absorbed by the entire cast and even with one rehearsal, it was absorbed by me. Each time I danced that ballet, I felt lucky to have seen that one rehearsal with him.

"Where are my glasses?" was the intermittent cry from Agnes DeMille, the well known American choreographer, when she was in rehearsal. The saga of the lost glasses, always found on the top of her head, became a memorable part of working with her. She gave us such clear images that one felt he was on a prairie with wild horses while rehearsing "Rodeo" or in Lizzie Borden's house when she rehearsed us in "Fall River Legend." Authentic movement was the most important aspect of a ballet to Agnes. Though she had her favorite dancers, she wanted authenticity from everyone; no fussy "put ons" for movement.

One could feel the cinematic vision in her work. Any of her ballets would have made a good movie. After all, her uncle was Cecil B. DeMille, the great Hollywood director.

The British choreographer Anthony Tudor prodded each of us in different, sometimes compromising ways. Often he would use the "shock" effect to get the reaction of drama and truth injected into his work. It was also often at the expense of the dancer's feelings. That was his whole point: bringing out feelings!

One of my great privileges was to be cast in his ballet, "Dark Elegies." This work, about the death of children and sung to German lieder, was the only ballet in the repertoire that was accorded the privacy of performance with no one allowed to watch from the wings. This ballet was different from all the others in that its subject matter created a very somber atmosphere. The coordination of costumes, lighting, choreography and music perfectly captured the atmosphere of sadness. Each of us dancing the ballet was completely immersed in it. When asked afterward how well it went, we never really had an answer. I still visualize the baritone singing the ballet downstage left, bathed in a spotlight.

Performing Harold Lander's ballet, "Etudes," was the test for the technique in all of us. I was always happy when that ballet would accompany us on tour. Though one felt he was doing class in front of the audience, the rehearsals were especially good for working on technique. It was also a constant crowd pleaser. During this first tour, I was having the big experience of my young career. I was learning everything I thought I needed in order to advance my career. By the end of the tour nine weeks later, I truly felt a part of the company.

During the long layoff period, when we would collect unemployment compensation, one had the chance to improve his technique with extra classes, unimpeded by rehearsals. Such short periods always resulted in improvement. It was also a time to catch up on letter writing and for doing things familial. I found an apartment that was a much better fit for Linda and me, and then some! It was the parlor floor on West 71st St. and West End Avenue. Among its many charms were ten- foot ceilings, hand carved oak walls, parquet flooring and Fleur de Lis fireplaces.

The apartment was 100 feet long. The upstairs neighbor was the lovely Broadway actress Blythe Danner and her scriptwriter husband Bruce Paltrow. Across the street lived the Motown composers, Holland, Dozier and Holland. The street was a dead end and usually quiet except when the Supremes, the Temptations, Ashford and Simpson or other Motown groups pulled up in their limos. I left the windows open then! The first thing I did after moving in was to write a letter to Linda about the apartment. She would be home from tour in two weeks time. I knew she would love the new place.

Among the offerings for the first New York Season at the Brooklyn Academy of Music was the great American choreographer Jerome Robbins' ballet, "Les Noces." I was, at last, going to finally meet and work with him. He cast me in the part of the Bed Warmer. This extraordinary work about the Russian peasant wedding ceremony was personally rehearsed by Mr. Robbins. After he became famous and wealthy from his Broadway shows, it was rare for him to appear personally for a rehearsal of one of his ballets. He came several times to work with us on "Les Noces."

During one fifteen-minute break, he had me go over my sequence repeatedly. He was intent on having me focus where he thought I should focus. I was focusing where he told me to. The two of us began to disagree. The tension was palpable. Finally the ballet master stopped the sequence repetition and asked me to look down. When I did the right eyelid stayed up creating an illusion of focusing elsewhere. It was later revealed during an optometrist visit that the elevator muscle in that eye was contracted. It was easily rectified by minor surgery. That pretty much exemplifies the detail in the work of Jerome Robbins. When it came to dancing, he missed nothing. Whenever I am asked what it was like to work with him, I think mostly of that one fifteen minute break!

That ballet was the highlight of the season, one I certainly would remember. The even more eagerly awaited event of that season was the partnership of Fracci and Bruhn. In "Giselle" and "Coppelia" they were unmatched; box office was never better than when they danced. To Lucia Chase they were her Fonteyn and Nureyev. These stars gave much excitement to the audience and the dancers. Fracci became everyone's favorite Romantic ballerina. Bruhn was just then passing his peak as the world's finest ballet classicist.

During the following season, which was danced at the New York State Theatre in Lincoln Center, Jose Limon, Mexico's greatest choreographer, came to work with us on his dance, "The Traitor," a work based on Christ and his disciples at the last supper. Alvin Ailey, the well known black choreographer, began a new work titled "The River" with original score by Duke Ellington. All three of these artists went out on tour with us as we prepared for the next New York season.

I performed one of Christ's twelve Disciples in Limon's work. Working with Limon was more profound than dancing one of his ballets. He was the only person I ever knew who was actually God-like; even his perspiration smelled wonderful. The harder he worked the better he smelled! Everyone noticed it. His manner was always congratulatory and his spirit for dancing was reverent. Though his ballet was better performed by his company, it was our honor to have a go at it.

When the "Duke" (he did not like to be called Mr. Ellington) arrived in the morning after company class, he would give the pianist sheet music. One day I was at the piano when he came in. I asked him when it was that he wrote the music he brought in each day. I was interested in his work pattern. It was rare for us to be working with a living composer who was creating a new composition for us to dance. "I never know Bob, it can happen at three in the morning so I keep my little electric keyboard next to my bed and input what comes to me in my sleep." I imagined him doing that and fixing up the loose ends before coming to let us hear it in the mornings.

Ellington was the ultimate gentleman. He was very respectful of the dancers, sensing he was on some sacred ground that he was not totally familiar with. As he watched the choreography unfold, depicting the various titles of running water (Falls, Vortex, Stream, *etc.)* complimenting the different sections of his music, he became more interested in the process at hand. He was used to working with musicians, not dancers.

He remained on tour until the piece was finished and attended the premiere at the Kennedy Center in Washington. It was commonly thought that the four of us, who danced the solo sections depicting "Falls," had some of his best music to dance to. Though he did not comment likewise, I often wondered if he didn't think so too. The ballet was very successful for everyone involved. The Duke did one more work for ABT before he passed away the following year. When I think of him I mostly remember his humble, natural way with us.

In the summer of 1970, ABT toured Europe for six weeks. Opening night was danced at Covent Garden, London, England with the Royal Family in attendance. During the final ballet of the evening, rain seeped through the stage area roofing, intensifying as the final curtain fell. Very wet, we greeted Queen Elizabeth II onstage after the performance. As we bowed and curtsied to her, she promised to have repairs completed for the following night's performance. I recall how collected she was in her embarrassment. Her promise complete, we kept dry for the remaining performances.

On the final day in England four of us awakened early to take up the offer of a Mr. H.L. Goode, a balletomane, to spend the afternoon at his Estate in Surrey. He picked us up in his silver Rolls Royce at the stage door. The carpet in this car was mink! The sound of the engine reminded one of the sounds of a human heart beating, only much softer. Each of us in turn had a chance to drive the vehicle. A perfect lunch served in the Manor house by polite servants and a ride through Surrey on the way back to London completed a rather extraordinary experience that the rest of the company had slept through.

Several festivals and cities later, we were becoming experienced with the phenomenon of the "raked" stages of European performance halls. The deep slant of the stage lowers toward the audience. This, so that the audience, seated slanted in the opposite direction, has the best possible view. At first this plays havoc with the dancer's equilibrium. Imagine dancers dancing on such an incline and you have the sensation of them constantly trying to keep or change their sense of balance.

Verona, Italy was the home of Romeo and Juliet whose graves are to the left of the entrance into the Arena di Verona. This vast arena is where we danced for three performances led by the Carla Fracci. She was the country's ballet icon. One could purchase FRACCI candy on every corner. Opening night offered "Giselle" with Fracci and Bruhn. Looking out into the arena we saw thousands of lit candles. As the orchestra began to play, the audience began to blow out the candles. Gradually their light disappeared, officially signaling the beginning of the performance. This magical tradition happened at each of our succeeding performances.

A post- performance party was given by Fracci and her husband, stage director Beppe Menegatti. We were taken to an enormous dining room atop a monastery which overlooked the Aldige River. From the table one could view the river and much of Verona through the arched portals so familiar in Italian architecture. The atmosphere in that room has never quite been matched again. The lighting, celestial period music led by live musicians and the abundance of food, wine, flowers and wall tapestries all combined to bring us back to the fourteenth century. It was totally successful. Miss Fracci added to the total effect by rendering a very good facsimile of Juliet herself, sitting there at the head of our table.

The final stop on the tour was the Herod Atticus Theatre in Athens, Greece. Our four days and nights there are remembered for two main events: swimming for our lives in the Mediterranean Sea and dancing with the Greeks until three in the morning at the Placa (late night gathering area near the Acropolis).

On a free afternoon Dennis, a fellow dancer, and I boarded a bus from Constitution Square, in the heart of Athens. We wanted to visit the Glyfada (Greek word for beach). It was thirty five miles away. Upon arrival at the sea, we rented surf boards for the afternoon. Promptly, we fell asleep on the boards in the noonday sun. Waking and looking around, I saw only ocean line. I had remembered a huge boulder jutting out of the water but I couldn't see it. I woke Dennis. He panicked, telling me he did not know how to swim. I thought he was joking until he slipped off the board and bobbed up and down several times. I remembered, from my life guard training by the Marines on Okinawa, that drowning people tend to climb the one who is trying to save them. As Dennis began to climb me I had to shock him by striking his jaw, just short of knocking him out. I managed to get him on the board and told him to hug it. As my luck would have it, at the end of his board was a brass ring and at the end of mine was a rope. Tying the boards together, I began to breaststroke our way back, praying that I was in the right direction.

It had gotten dark and rain had begun to fall. It seemed like hours before I saw that boulder again. I then realized that we were going to make it back to shore! Suddenly I gained renewed strength and got us to where Dennis could stand in the water chest high. I fainted on the shoreline. I regained consciousness to the sounds of a lady yelling at us in Greek; we had not given her enough money to have stayed on the boards all day long! It was ten p.m. The curtain for the ballet was 9 p.m.

We hitchhiked back to Athens, arriving as the final ballet was beginning. We had missed the entire performance and, without questions being asked, were fined and put on notice to be addressed by the Union when we got back to New York. No one wanted to know why we were absent. They wouldn't have believed us anyway.

We suddenly felt revitalized, full of energy. It was the strangest feeling after all that sun and exhaustion. We joined other dancers at the Placa, the place where we were sure Anthony Quinn filmed his famous 'dancing with the table in his teeth' scene from "Zorba the Greek." The music, men dancing with men and everyone drinking Ouzo all matched the film perfectly. We all stayed until 3am, doing more than a little dancing of our own.

Given open tickets back to the USA, I made arrangements to meet Linda in Barcelona, Spain. She had just arrived for another lengthy tour with the Harkness Ballet. The flamenco, the ramblas (outdoor eating and gathering area), the bullfights and Antonio Gaudi's architecture insured that this was a city to fall in love with, especially if the two people were in love.

We had an exceptionally good time together. On the final day before I had to return to New York and leave her again, we strolled and shopped, stopping at Eva's Boutique just for the heck of it. This store was THE fashion spot on the continent. Movie stars, sports figures and Mrs. Harkness shopped there. Linda caught the eye of the House Designer. He invited her into his couture room, telling her he loved to dress dancers. Within minutes he was draping chocolate colored velvet shawls with ostrich feathers up and down her frame. He remarked that anything would look good on her. Browsing around, I found a rack of fur coats. I pulled one out. The tag on the coat read Paul Newman. I tried it on. The designer shouted, "You have to have that!" It was a double breasted fox coat comprising thirty-two pelts of Zorro fox from South America. "It is too big for Newman. It won't need cutting for you. Take it!" he yelled. I would have taken it in a moment but I did not have money to pay for it. He wanted four hundred dollars and told me to send it to him when I got home. Was he for real? Was Paul Newman expecting this coat? Was this a "hot" item? Was he HOPING to get rid of it?

I made a decision to take his offer and, of course, wired

him the money upon my return to New York. Over the next few years, I did not hear from any authorities in either Barcelona or South America so I decided the designer was honest after all. I can recall that, especially during the next decade while fur was still considered acceptable wear, the coat not only kept me warm but was the topic of conversation whenever I wore it. Once, on a New York bus, I was offered twenty-five hundred dollars for it. It was a magnificent item. Thirty-five years and several linings later, the coat was recently given to Charity. I often wondered if Newman ended up with a fur coat after all.

Linda's creation would not be ready for a week. I would have to wait until she returned to New York to see her in it. When she later wore it to a performance of the Metropolitan Opera, I felt that the designer would have appreciated his creation; particularly winning was the fact that the color of the velvet and Linda's eyes matched perfectly. What a memory that was, what a guy he was and what a girl she was!

I was very much in love with her. Our time together in Barcelona solidified our feelings. I could feel the closeness between us. She was pure of heart and mysterious at the same time. The more I got to know her the more I wanted to know. I sensed I would never get to know her totally. She had a very large capacity for loving and for being loved.

I also sensed how much she was enjoying her time with the Harkness Company, the trips to Europe and her lifestyle in general. Though she was absolutely serious about making the most of each day dancing, she did not take herself too seriously. She took her work seriously; her intent was always clearly centered.

It would be too bad if these long separations would allow another person to get inside this relationship. Though I knew that would not happen on my end, was I taking a huge risk on her end? How much risk would I be willing to take?

A Major Change

The John F. Kennedy Center for the Performing Arts in Washington, DC opened on September 9, 1971. ABT had been named the Center's official ballet company and we were slated to dance on opening night. The dance union had been gaining strength within ballet companies, mostly correcting adverse working conditions. One of those conditions was dancing on hard (tongue and groove over cement) stages. Five of us along with the Union representative of the company were asked to try out different experimental flooring that would eventually be required of any future buildings where professional dance was presented. The result was a basket weave sprung floor. The lasting effect of better flooring for professional dancers can be measured by those of us who still have our original hips.

On opening night at the Center, during the ballet "Etudes," the hem of the scrim at the rear of the stage broke open. Loaded down with a million bbs to hold it taut, the stage was suddenly rolling with metal bbs. Only a ballerina the likes of Lupe Serrano would finish her variation dancing on bbs! Before her partner called for the curtain, the entire orchestra was bombarded. The sound of the bbs hitting the instruments did, indeed, have something in common with the ballet's score by Czerny. Apart from this major disruption, the opening night and the rest of the first season at the Center were successful. ABT and the Center looked to be a good fit.

The toured continued. Finally we were flying most places and staying longer at each stop. We were also visiting the largest cities in the country. Being in love and knowing that only by being in the same company could our relationship develop, I decided to propose a major change. I no longer wanted to let chance play a role. Other people entered our lives. My reaction to that was simple. I did not want to know about "him" unless he was better for her than I was. Then she should have him. She deserved the best there was. However, I wasn't willing to risk anymore.

I presented my dilemma to Lucia Chase. She agreed to take Linda into the company even though "we are full up!" Linda was in Berlin, Germany, starring in the Harkness Ballet's film version of Walter Gore's ballet "Eaters of Darkness." It was the first professional dance video, sold as the leader film on the M*A*S*H television series home video.

I called Berlin from Kansas City. Excitedly, I told her of my plans for us: that I loved her, that I wanted to marry her and that Lucia had agreed to give her a contract. SILENCE! Demurely, she reminded me she was already on contract and that she could not break it. She told me that she also loved me but that she was not ready to be married. REJECTION! The timing was off. Did I come across with too much immediacy? I realized that I would have to wait until she was ready. The following morning, at the hotel's breakfast room, Lucia came over to my table and asked, "Why the long face?" After explaining Linda's reaction, Lucia encouragingly responded, "Bob, you have a real 'pro' there. Things are going to work out for you, you'll see." I decide to relax about "us." I felt that I had done what I could to do. I also sensed that Lucia was right.

In the spring, we began the next New York season at the Metropolitan Opera House. It was during this season that I was asked to dance the role of "Albrecht" in "Giselle" with the Fokine Ballet on Long Island. Igor Youskevitch, the great Albrecht of the early ABT days, was going to supervise the production. Working with him made all the difference to me. Igor's huge reputation preceded him into the studio. We were alone for our first rehearsal. He spoke about the role and how enthralled Count Albrecht was with the peasant girl he watched from high atop his castle. How Albrecht was frustrated that his station in life prevented him from getting to know her. How he had to finagle a way to do that. Igor remembered how he felt dancing the part, especially when he got to the peasant village in disguise and immediately fell in love with her.

Igor was becoming Albrecht as he spoke; "I didn't mean to break her heart. She was so lovely. I thought I could, for just an afternoon, pretend to be someone I was not. Then she suddenly died in my arms and I could not rest until I visited her grave to tell her how very, very sorry I was for having deceived her." Life was imitating art; I could so easily feel Albrecht's love for Giselle.

In loafer shoes and street clothes, Igor began the simple pas de deux of the first act, going onto the daisy scene and then responding to her falling before him. It was all there. I had seen it tens of times with ABT but I had never really seen it before now. Igor made quite an impression on me. He gave the essence of the character to me. He made Albrecht human.

The following rehearsals focused on the manner in which one danced the steps of the ballet. When Anna, my Giselle, joined us, he also demonstrated Giselle's part. Anna was a dancer with the Met Opera Ballet and perfectly typecast for the role of Giselle. Igor went on to make much of Albrecht's second act variation, again telling his thoughts as he danced. Such nuance gave way to *port de bras (*carriage of the arms) I had not seen in the role before. Was this the way it was danced originally, head in forearm during the *chassé (*chase) into the *tours en l'air (*full body turns in the air)? It certainly conveyed the impression of grief. We were captivated. For this romantic period ballet, he seemed the authentic Albrecht. We wished we could have seen him onstage.

  The Fokine Ballet performances occurred in the middle of the Met season. I was working around performances at Lincoln Center to rehearse with Igor. I found the role to be challenging but with Igor's help, I thought I could get very much inside of it. That happened during the third and final performance.

  I began to think of moving on from ABT. The short tour of Europe left me with a very good impression of the continent. We had all heard of the ballet companies there and of the good contracts. We had also heard of the lazy dancers. In European ballet companies, one is contracted until the age of forty. Then one has a lifetime pension. One has comforts that go along with security. Therefore, for most of the dancers there is not much reason to be motivated by the work. As a late starter who had missed some valuable time, I was doing very well but if I wanted to dance principal roles often, I needed to think where that could best happen. At ABT there were too many ambitious dancers who were ahead of me.

A call from Andre Eglevsky asking me to dance in "Les Sylphides" with the Eglevsky Ballet was my next surprise during the Met Season. Andre was another Ballets Russes dancer. He spent the latter half of his career as Balanchine's leading dancer. The performances were scheduled for the last week of August on the island of Nantucket, Massachusetts. He agreed to rehearse me in the part.

In a very different way from Igor, rehearsals with Andre were wonderful. The main difference was in the personalities of the two men. Both were of the same era but danced very differently. Igor's type was romantic. Andre was vigorously virile. During the *arabesque* turns of the Poet's variation, there appeared the same *port de bra* Igor showed for Albrecht's *tour en l'airs*. The "style" of the era was again apparent!

Back at the New York apartment, there was a letter from Linda. She would be arriving from Europe on the morning of my first performance with Eglevsky. I thought she would like to see the performance. "Les Sylphides" was her favorite ballet. I left her a note on the dining room table with details.

During the morning rehearsal my partner, Diane, from the Pennsylvania Ballet, fell during her variation. An x-ray revealed a severe fracture. Andre was trying not to scratch the ballet but it looked like he would have no other choice. One did not have understudies for guest artists and it was too late to fly in a replacement from New York.

Linda called the theatre from the Nantucket airstrip. Andre asked one of the dancers to pick up Linda. Unbeknown to me, Andre was going to ask Linda to replace my injured partner. Meanwhile, he had me go through my variation once more, perfecting what he liked best about the steps.

Linda was one of Andre's favorite dancers. He was aware that we were a couple but not that she would be coming to the performance. Everyone knew that the Harkness Ballet was in Europe. Her driver prepared Linda by asking if she had her pointe shoes with her. Of course she did! Dancers always carry their equipment with them. By the time she arrived at the theatre, she was acclimated to the idea of dancing her favorite ballet with the man she said she loved for an admiring director on a fabulous island off the Atlantic. Jet lag? She didn't have time for it.

We had sufficient time for a costume fitting and rehearsal. She knew the ballet well. Of course, this is one of our fondest memories. The entire cast seemed elevated by the circumstances surrounding this performance. Linda looks back on it as one of the most enjoyable performances of her career. There is nothing quite like being the one who saves the day!

And so the summer of '72 was the time when many things came together and others began to take root. By the end of the Kennedy Center season that fall, I decided not to renew my contract with ABT. It was time for a major change. I was twenty seven years old and I wanted to be a "Prince."

"Don Quixote" Rehearsal

On My Own

I had performances lined up with the Edward Villella Ensemble for the winter/spring months. Villella was a star of the New York City Ballet. When his schedule permitted, he culled a group of dancers together. The dates were sporadic allowing for great flexibility. If one were busy elsewhere, he was quite easily replaced for any of the Villella performances. Villella's ensemble danced mostly on the east coast and more specifically in upstate New York and New Jersey. His was a set pattern; three of the same Balanchine ballets in between which he danced two pas de deux. It sold well and it paid well.

After just a few performances with the Ensemble, I received a call from James Moore, assistant ballet master at ABT. He was moving to Stockholm to take over the directorship of the Royal Swedish Ballet. He asked me to join him there as a principal dancer. The offer took me by surprise. I told him that I would think about it. He replied by sending a roundtrip ticket for me to go to Sweden over the Christmas holidays.

Stockholm in December is not the brightest spot on the Earth. Things got off to a dismal start when I arrived at 1 p.m. and found that it was totally dark outside. Still, I found the people intriguing. I surmised that, given so little daylight, they would have to be. I quickly became enamored with the thatched roofs on some of the older buildings near Skansen and the feast of St. Lucia celebration which was as charming as it was old.

The following morning I took the company class. It was filled with mostly older dancers and one beautiful young girl whom everyone was talking about, inside and outside of Stockholm. Her name was Annika and she was the company ballerina. Observing the level of the dancers', I felt that Moore really needed not only me but several others as well. The dancer's lack of energy was very evident. The canteen was a far more interesting place to be. I think that is where they spent most of their time in the theatre.

The vast repertoire had been built up by previous directors and, of course, the opera house had a venerable reputation. Within a few days, Linda joined me in Stockholm; funny how sunny Stockholm suddenly became! We planned to take a holiday on the Eurail (Europe's railway system) that would take us the length of the continent from Stockholm to Lisbon.

After watching performances, it was clear to both of us that this would not be the company for me. The timing was premature. Moore was disappointed when I told him I could not join him there. He hoped I would reconsider but also seemed to understand my point of view.

Our holiday was spectacular! More than once we were the only people in the train's cabin, sometimes in the whole of the car. The privacy of it, complete with our cheeses and wine, made for comforts more closely associated to hotel rooms! We made a stop in Gstaad, Switzerland, for Linda to introduce me to Mrs. Harkness' confidant, Connie Anderson. Connie was an American who was permanently living in Switzerland and who had grown very close to the Harkness dancers. Linda also wanted very much for me to meet a chap named "Mr. Brassel" who managed the local Credit Suisse Bank. We spent a few days there enjoying the chalet atmosphere and the lovely cooking. We even enjoyed being awakened by the cow bells.

Mr. Brassel told me about my Swiss ancestors to the north, in a town called St. Margarethen. There I would find Brassel

Shulhaus (shoe store) as well as Brasselstrasse (street), *et al.* There the name was as common as Smith was in the USA. I was amazed to learn that! During our travels as a young family we never found another exact spelling of our surname. It became a game in each new city to find a telephone book and look in it to see if there was another Brassel. Years later, I did that game again as a dancer. I didn't succeed then either. They were all in St. Margarethen!

Back in New York, I spent a couple of weeks at the Harkness House for Ballet Arts, while the company was rehearsing before they began their States tour. I took company class and watched rehearsals. I was interested to see what they were like. Though New York had not seen this company perform, the word on the dancers was very good indeed.

Linda and I began to talk seriously about my joining the Harkness Ballet. Though considered a step below professionally, it could be a step up in other ways. For one thing, it could seal our relationship and there would then be time to discuss working together in a more classical repertoire somewhere else, perhaps in Europe. On more than one occasion we had discussed Linda dancing the classical repertoire. I gave the notion of joining Harkness some serious thought.

On a particularly lovely spring evening in New York, after an equally enjoyable day together, we found ourselves walking home holding hands. We did little talking the whole of West

72nd St. Once inside the apartment, sharing cognac, Linda told me that she thought it was time. Time? I had every urge to stretch this one out. I did, a little. And then, there in the living room on West 71st St. she said she felt the time was right for us to get married.

Our tight schedules pinpointed a wedding date for the third Saturday in August. The day after the wedding we would fly with the Harkness Ballet to Santo Domingo for a week's performances. It would also serve as our honeymoon. Before the wedding, Linda had a five week tour of Europe scheduled and I had been contracted to teach several master classes in Texas as well as in my hometown of Buffalo, NY. I was interested in teaching though I felt that I had too little experience to be taken seriously. I thought of those young boys I taught at Ft. Bragg. That was about all I had behind me; them and the colonel's daughters!

The wedding took place in Linda's hometown of Somerville, Massachusetts. This was the only chance for her parents to throw the "big" party. They had little time to organize it; telephone calls to me in Texas asking if we wanted chicken or steak, how many invitations did we need for people they did not know, did we want a certain type of music for the ceremony/reception? It was all enough to cause heartburn which I am sure it did. They didn't even know if I knew how to "dance" with her! In a later conversation with her daughter, Linda's Mother said she knew, of course, that he knows HOW to dance but "Does he REALLY know how to dance?" Imagine the embarrassment of it all if Arthur Murray hadn't been there for me all those years earlier!

We took care of the church music when we got to Massachusetts the week of the wedding. The beautiful Somerset Louis XIV Ballroom on Commonwealth Avenue in downtown Boston was the sight of the reception. A glowing memory is the moment when, to our surprise, the entire wall of mirrors ascended for our entrance. The Viennese orchestra began playing a Strauss Waltz for me to take up my bride and show the people how ballet dancers REALLY dance! That moment had more than a touch of theatre in it. Today, those who were in attendance still remind us that ours was the very best wedding they ever attended. It must have been the dancing!

The reality of being married was wonderful! Linda was twenty-seven and I was twenty-eight. Being with her on the layoff periods was the best of times. We had time, money and each other. It was also time to socialize with friends and neighbors and to enjoy New York. The thought of spending the rest of our lives together was euphoric.

My contract with the Harkness Ballet was signed before the wedding. I would use the Santo Domingo trip to rehearse and watch the ballets I was learning. After a lengthy rehearsal period in New York, the company would begin a five week US tour and then, after a brief layoff, another rehearsal period before a ten week tour of Europe and the Middle East. At last, my chance to see what those incredible Harkness tours were like. Everyone in the dance world wanted to experience that.

During our Christmas break, we danced in Manila, the Philippines. The modern dance choreographer, Norman Walker, invited us to be the guest artists at the Cultural Center there. He was very fond of Linda's work, having choreographed for her at the Harkness Ballet. We would dance the Sugar Plum Fairy and the Nutcracker Prince in the local company's production of the holiday classic as well as "Les Sylphides." Walker's ballets would be danced by the Philippine dancers during the ten day run. When the time came to depart for Manila, neither of us thought to check the airline tickets that had been sent to us by the Philippine impresario. Such details were not normally our concern.

We very soon learned that were flying to Manila via EUROPE! This thirty-seven hour trip, involving eleven layovers and airplanes, stopped in Paris, Athens, Karachi, Bombay, Calcutta and points in between before landing in Manila. On some flights we were the only people aboard, just us and six stewardesses and stewards. We felt like cargo! This extraordinary flight schedule had to have an explanation. That revelation came when we met the impresario, husband to the Philippine dance company's director, in Manila. He told us that the trip saved him money! We learned our lesson. We also felt very tired for a long time; partially made up for by the wonderful accommodations provided for us in the director's home complete with maid service and fresh papaya each morning.

Irmgard and Diana surprised us with a visit from Okinawa for the opening night's performance. It had been six years since we had seen each other. She looked wonderful and was elated at meeting Linda. She was even more impressed with the performance. A lady of courage and strength, she told me of Ted's failing health and that she foresaw moving to Washington State when his latest tour of duty was complete. As we saw them off at the airport the following day, I felt very glad that we saw each other again. She gave me every sense that she was very happy for me. One never really forgets such a person or experience.

Our Philippine impresario had another surprise for us. He had only one ticket for us to depart on; only one of us would get back to the USA timely. Again he cried financial troubles. I was beginning to feel lucky that we received our full fees. I explained to him that we could not leave the Philippine separately as we were contracted to dance "The Nutcracker" in Red Bank, New Jersey, in two days time. A phone call later, he produced two tickets for us as far as Amsterdam, Holland. He would give us a letter to present to the president of the KLM Dutch airlines, explaining who we were, what our plight was and that, due to harsh financial circumstances in Manila would he please consider allowing us to fly to Newark, New Jersey

GRATIS? We took the letter. At the very least we would make it to the European continent!

This craziness, clearly a legal matter begging to be heard, continued when the KLM president AGREED to do what was requested of him! I would believe it when I saw the Newark tarmac, which I did six hours later. So much for wonderful papayas!

Upon arriving in Newark, New Jersey, we went directly to the Paper Mill Playhouse where we danced that night in the New Jersey Ballet's production of "The Nutcracker." We had made it! I wanted to have a serious talk with Norman Walker, who represented us for the Manila appearances, as soon as I could but I would first have to find out why I was scratching so much. I felt about forty-five years old and as though I weighed about four hundred pounds.

I had begun itching on the flight from Amsterdam. At a dermatologist's office the morning after the New Jersey Ballet performance, I learned that I had a case of the Shingles. My "cool" wife had taken the recent events in her customary, calm style. She seemed less overtly affected, though clearly perturbed, by them. My weaker condition reflected the concern I felt for both of us as well as the people at the Paper Mill Playhouse. I later realized that her calm demeanor was really a reaction to my reactions. This was to become our habit as a married couple. As in so many lasting marriages, this interaction continually works both ways.

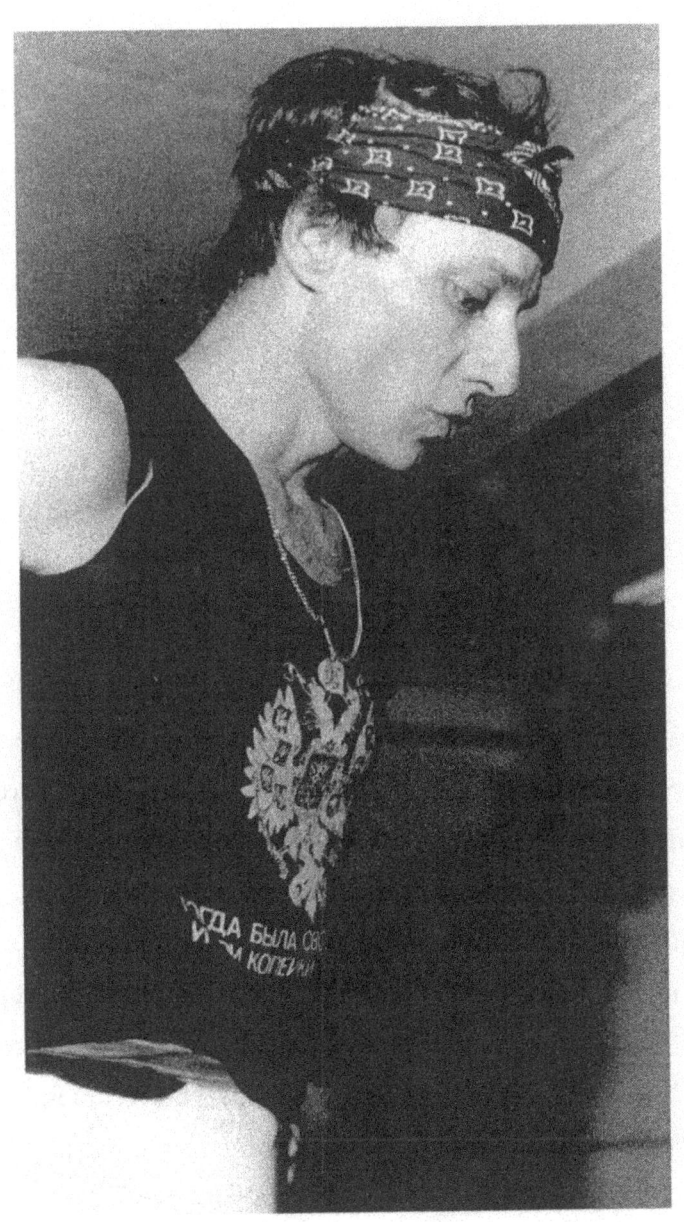

Contemplating a difficult step

A Most Extraordinary Tour

Back in New York, my initial rehearsal period offered me the roles of the Prince in "Firebird" and the *pas de deux*, "Three Preludes." The latter work, by British choreographer Ben Stevenson, had recently won the first gold medal awarded for choreography at the famous Varna Ballet Competition in Bulgaria. I learned this ballet with Linda. It was the first *pas de deux* of our fifteen year stage partnership. We danced together in the "Firebird" also, she taking the role of the Princess. A new ballet was also in the making. The choreography was by Margo

Sappington with an original score by Michael Kamen. Its inspiration came from the sculptures of Auguste Rodin. Sappington wanted to see Rodin's work "move." Margo and I had danced together in the Joffrey Company. She cast me in the "Burghers of Calais" section of her new ballet. Linda danced "Eternal Spring."

Vienna, Austria was the first stop on the tour. The city of Mozart, Spanish riding horses and feathered hotel beds, Vienna was also a huge center for dance. The Harkness Ballet was Europe's favorite American ballet company. The company appeared there every year and the continent was very familiar with them.

A trip to the Spanish riding horses, in quarters that resembled a castle, reminded all of us what rhythm was about. Here were animals performing *cabrioles* (joining of the heels in mid air) and *pirouettes* to the strains of Strauss waltzes. I particularly liked watching the horses enter the gilded ring in cadence, without music. They truly represented Austrian aristocracy!

My first performance with the company went well. I danced "Firebird" in Vienna. This production, by Canadian choreographer Brian Macdonald, was especially theatrical and thoroughly captured the magic of Stravinsky's score. The company did not work nearly as hard during the day as ABT did on tour. Though the dancers were excellent, this was an entirely different atmosphere. The repertoire consisted mainly of one act ballets.

The big, classical ballets took up a lot of our time at ABT. Here everyone seemed to be on the same page as to the quality of the time they spent. The repeated European travel had trained them about life quality on the continent. I was impressed.

If this tour were scripted it would include not only Spanish riding horses, feathered beds and wiener schnitzel in Austria but also the crown jewels of Iran, the gypsy camps, mosques and hammans (public baths) of Turkey, a near re-acquaintance with Ella Fitzgerald in the ancient ruins of Lebanon and a war in Greece.

Istanbul was the tour's most mysterious city. The minarets of the mosques rang out with prayer five times a day. This caused a momentary cessation in activity; all citizens on their knees, joining in the prayer. That was a risk taking event when one was riding in a taxi and the driver stopped to pay homage.

While entering the Blue Mosque, a tour guide approached us to ask if he could show us the sights. His English was very good and his manner more than acceptable. He explained the hundreds of carpets in the huge mosques; their derivations and symbolizations. He then insisted that we experience the Turkish baths and an authentic Turkish dinner afterwards.

We separated at the hammans, the girls going into the smaller section of the public baths. They weren't sure they would partake but wanted to see the inside. Once inside the larger section, we did not have a choice in the matter. It was understood why you were there; to have your entire body scrubbed clean. This was not a tourist spot. The scrub was more like a beating with long, soapy brooms as we lay naked, head to toe on a circular marble slab. The slab sloped inwards in the middle from the thousands of bodies that have been on them over the hundreds of years. I heard one or more yelps from my colleagues as sumo wrestler types wielded their soapy brooms on us. The feeling was more like a serious tingle than pain. Then we were individually placed in circular stainless steel tubes that sprayed water in all directions. Afterwards, while wearing Turkish robes and sipping tea, we felt the refreshing, softer tingling effect of the bath technique. We rested with that feeling while we finished the tea. The girls were waiting for us as we exited the baths, anxious to hear of the experience. After listening to us they were sure that they wanted no part of the hammans. We, however, felt like the day was new and that our bodies were totally rested. The hammans were clearly something to keep in mind.

  The guide promised us a visit to the Gypsy camps after the evening performance, asking only for a ticket to the ballet in return. He watched from the first row as we all experienced a magical "Firebird" lit entirely in gold at Istanbul's magnificent outdoor arena. That was the Turkish "take" on our lighting cues. Apparently, they liked the way gold light reflected on their stonewalled backdrop.

Following the performance, the guide had two cars waiting for us. The ballet master joined us for the ride to the Gypsies. There at the top of the city was a row of huts, each with naked light bulbs shining from them. The guide took us to the second to last hut. As we followed him to the backroom, we passed cubicles on the left and the right; one had love making activity, one had eating activity, one was for the animals and one was for sleeping.

Earth served as their flooring. In our room were seated four musicians with instruments we had never seen before. They were made of tin and their particular shapes offered their individual sounds; one was an upside down wash pan used as a hand drum, another was a scrub board played on with a steel pipe stick, two pans gently tapping each other worked as symbols and the fourth musician had made his harp from unraveled chicken wire attached to large tree branches that were slightly bent.

We took our seats on metal chairs in the purple ten foot by ten foot room. Suddenly three dancing gypsies entered the room, wearing only what looked like underwear, clanking hand chimes over their heads. Others entered with wine and cheese for us. We were about to be entertained and robbed at the same time! They danced, the music played and the naked light bulb flickered. Their attempts at taking the gold from our necks, wrists and fingers occurred as the dancing ladies danced to our laps. One, telling Linda that she was from Toledo, Ohio, was particularly aggressive at body picking. Their efforts were unsuccessful but we wanted to take care of them with some cash. Our trusting guide prevented us from giving too much money. "These are people who sell their babies!" he announced.

The following morning, while having breakfast on the veranda of our hotel, we read in the International Herald Tribune of the defection of the Kirov Ballet star, Mikhail Baryshnikov. As I gazed out over the Bosporus Sea, I remembered his brilliant performances at Festival Hall on the night ABT arrived in London several years earlier. His defection was big news for the international ballet world. Everyone hoped he would dance in America!

The flight from Istanbul to Beirut was troubled. To begin with, it seemed too crowded. Then, shortly after reaching cruising altitude, there was a huge drop in air pressure. Several people, whose seat belts were unfastened, were lifted to the plane's ceiling while others were sent flying out of the toilets. This was some air pocket! Several more times before landing, the plane felt like it was being shaken. That was just the beginning of "thrills" surrounding the Lebanese portion of the tour. It was 1974. The country was at war.

Upon arrival we were taken to a row of taxis that would transport us to Baalbeck, fifty kilometers away from the military tensions in Beirut. We were scheduled to rehearse that afternoon among the ancient ruins there. All twenty taxis were huge 1960s Buicks and Chevrolets. The drivers drove at breakneck speed on a two lane highway. They were bent on seeing which of them would arrive first. Anxious to hear about America, our driver turned his head to us in the backseat while keeping pedal to floor. "You see Yogi Berra and Empire State building?" How big Hollywood?" I grabbed his head, turning his face toward the road. His English was fair enough to listen to our answers and keep his eyes on the road at the same time! If his antics continued, I was certain we would not arrive without some kind of accident.

As it happened, he did sideswipe an oncoming vehicle. Suddenly we were all stopped at the roadside. In the oncoming vehicle was a Lebanese general who took our driver with him back to Beirut. We heard that they commonly hung people for such an offense! We split up into three of the cars behind us. As we were nearing the hotel, we noticed one of our soloists standing alongside the car she had been riding in; its engine sitting on the side of the road. We collected her and, by midday, were all miraculously accounted for at the hotel. We shared our wild stories about the taxi drivers!

Ella Fitzgerald, Joan Baez, Charlie Mingus and others were finishing a jazz /folk festival in the ancient ruins as we began a festival of our own. This spectacular outdoor theatre had all the professional lighting of any fully equipped indoor venue. The theatre was packed with audiences from May through September.

Huge gold-colored stone columns, each thirty feet high, were somehow balanced one upon the other hundreds and hundreds of years ago. These columns were lined up next to each other surrounding the entire arena area. Atop the columns were ornate carvings resembling crowns. For centuries, architects the world over have tried to figure out just how the construction was achieved. It was an overwhelming and beautiful sight. At night, with the lights glowing on the columns, one imagined a Hollywood set. The Sappington/Kamen ballet was premiered there and immediately became the audience favorite. I don't think that ballet ever had a better setting, not even at the Champs Elysee Theatre in Paris, across the street from the Rodin museum itself, where we gave our final performance of the tour.

When it came time to return to Beirut for the flight to Athens, I took the company manager, Jeannot, aside. I wanted the company to travel differently. I wanted a bus or a helicopter, anything but Lebanese taxi drivers. Assuring me that the accident could never happen again and certainly not to the same people, I agreed to go in a taxi. As we walked up to the car, I opened the front seat door, indicating for Jeannot to get in. He would be riding WITH us! He smiled and got into the car.

Ten minutes from the airport, with me again sitting behind

the driver, I saw the crash coming. It was immediate but I found time to grab Linda's hand and raise it up to the car ceiling; my gesture to the fact that this time we would be killed. Though the damage was actually less than the previous accident and no one was actually killed, our nerves were frayed. Jeannot's expression as our eyes met accented the fact that this was way too dangerous to ever do again. We would need HELICOPTERS! The driver managed to get us to the airport twenty minutes before the flight departed for Athens, not enough time for a scotch on the rocks which we all could have used.

We flew uneventfully to Athens, Greece. It was very interesting to be back in Athens at the same theatre with a different company. I made sure we all got to the Placa and that everyone stayed away from the Glyfada. On the day we were to depart for Paris, Linda and I picked up a pair of pants that had been tailored for me. Upon arriving at the shop, the tailor asked "Aren't you dancers from the Harkness Ballet? How are you going to leave Athens?" The tailor was referring to the fact that war with Cyprus had broken out hours earlier. Was he JOKING?

As we left his shop we saw women running through the streets carrying sacks of potatoes. There weren't any men insight! We hurried back to the hotel to find the company dancers and others guests huddled in the lobby. Women were behind the bar serving drinks. We heard news reports about the combat and that all boarders were closed. One of our principal dancers was Turkish. Had the local authorities seen his passport, he would have been taken away. During this ordeal, Jeannot insisted he remain in his room.

Speculations were the order of the day, especially with the US Embassy employees trying to contact the Nixon administration in hopes that the White House would send Air Force planes to rescue them and their families. They, too, were milling around our lobby. After dinner, our company secretary placed a sign on the elevator door:

ALL HARKNESS DANCERS AND STAFF ARE TO BE IN THE LOBBY WITH LUGGAGE AT 7:00am SHARP. DO NOT ASK ANY QUESTIONS!!!!!!!!

Of course all the others wanted to know what that was all about. We retired for the evening wondering too. The secretary took her orders from Eduard, our tour manager. Eduard spoke twelve languages, was nearly seventy years old and had an extensive history of managing ballet companies. Having coffee with him one afternoon, he told me how he had seen all the great ballerinas. He knew one when he saw one. For him, Linda DiBona was one of them. He thought her "Le Corsair" *pas de deux* was right up there with the best. "The only 'best' there was for that ballet was Fonteyn. I like to watch Linda dance. She reminds me very much of Margot; same look, same quality!"

Getting onto a bus the following morning, we all agreed to "not ask any questions." It was far too early anyway! As the bus pulled away from the hotel several Americans waved us off. Their expressions were quite hopeless.

Eduard kept fifteen thousand dollars cash in his pocket. Rebekah Harkness made sure of that. Once into our bus trip, he explained that he was taking us to the port of Corinth where he had reserved cabins for us on the last luxury liner being allowed to leave the Greek port. We were sailing to Rimini, Italy. Eduard hadn't been around the "ballet tour" block for nothing!

Upon arrival in Rimini we saw the morning headlines. The International Herald Tribune covered the story on the front page: HARKNESS BALLET DANCERS STRANDED IN GREEK/CYPRIOT WAR! The Tribune did not yet know of our luxury liner escape.

In Rimini we ate a spectacular Italian meal while awaiting a chartered plane from London to take us to Paris. Even though all transportation in Italy was on strike (charter flights excepted!), Eduard came to the rescue again! We arrived in Paris in time to do the final three of six scheduled performances. It was our pleasure to spend the first afternoon perusing the Rodin Museum across the street from the theatre and, in the evening, to bring his sculptures to life on stage. I imagined the audience visiting the museum before they entered the theatre.

The public was very gracious about accepting us three

days late. I had not heard such ovations for a company's opening performance since ABT, and then only when the stars danced. The Sappington/Kamen ballet, entitled "Rodin Mis en Vie," again further solidified the company's reputation and brought thunderous applause. The Europeans loved this company and these dancers!

The tour was over. The Harkness dancers always wanted their tours to go on and on. Who would not miss seeing Eduard suddenly disappearing only to make an inspired entrance with news of some unforeseen happenstance, or living in luxury hotels with services one could so easily get used to; the chocolates on the pillows and the heated towel racks. And then there were always the audiences, those people of different countries and languages clapping wholeheartedly and wanting more? It was the same everywhere and the dancers knew their responsibility was to give them what they hoped for.

Upon returning to New York we caught up with the news that Rebekah's attorneys were again pressuring her to give up the company. Much of her wealth was down due to the previous year's oil embargo. The company was costing three million dollars a year without return on the money, year after year after year. It was then officially announced that the company would cease operations at the close of the winter's US tour.

Rebekah weakened. She had been ill off and on and probably had not been well for some time. It was unlikely that a

Board would be organized. Her reputation as a wealthy woman who ran the organization on her terms preceded her. Boards raised monies for companies without money. In the final months there were full-hearted attempts to help save the Harkness Ballet. Nothing worked. On March 1, 1975, the company gave its final performance at Dade County Auditorium, West Palm Beach, Florida.

The decade long era of the Harkness Ballet was ended. During that controversial decade, many dancers' careers were continued and /or begun, many ballets were made with various choreographers and musicians coming together, some for the first time, and the Harkness School for Ballet Arts was firmly established. Most importantly, however, was the special reputation of the company on the European continent. To date, no other American ballet company has enjoyed success there on the same scale. Its legacy would be indelible.

Age two with brother "Murph" (on left)   The author as a teenager

The Joffery Ballet, Jacob's Pillow 1965 (Brassel, top row, far left)

Specialist 5th Class Brassel, Sharpshooter: US Army

Rehearsing "The Sleeping Beauty," Act III with DiBona,
Photo: API

Rehearsal break with ABT colleagues, NY State Theatre, Lincoln Center

DiBona as "Kitri"

Brassel as "Prince Siegfried"

As Basilio in "Don Quixote"   Photo: Alan Bergman

As Spartacus with Virgie (DiBona)
Photo: Le Grand Theatre du Charleroi

As Adam in "After Eden"   Photo: Michel Lidvac

The Author with his son Matthew, age three
Photo: Bosworth

Dancing Together

During the next few months, we considered taking advantage of living and working abroad. As we were contemplating a trip to Europe, we met Jeanne Brabants, Director of the Ballet vanVlaanderen in Antwerp, Belgium. She was observing Elena Tchernichova's professional class at the Harkness House for Ballet Arts. Following the closing of the company, we had been spending time there and elsewhere taking classes and rehearsing for various guest appearances.

    Brabants offered us principal contracts with her company

We did some research and found that she had established an exceptionally well reputed ballet school in Antwerp, out of which grew her company. Though the contemporary repertoire was not what we were looking for, this did look to be an entry opportunity into the European dance scene for us. We accepted her offer. The only drawback was that I would be leaving my work with Elena. I was very interested in learning from her all that I could regarding the Vaganova (Russian) system of teaching ballet. In the period between the closing of the Harkness Ballet and our arriving in Antwerp, I worked with her consistently. I knew one day that my teaching would be based on this method. For now, I was still a dancer with time ahead of me for dancing.

We were excited at the opportunity of living and working in Europe. It was the beginning of a period that would make our careers quite different from those of most of our colleagues. The amount of traveling that we did harkened back to the days of the Diaghilev and the Ballets Russes era. All told, we danced in more than one hundred cities in twenty-five countries on five continents before we were in a semi-retirement position as directors of our own school and company in the United States.

The charming city of Antwerp, with its Sunday markets, cobblestone streets, wonderful chocolates, coffee and Belgian waffles, was also the diamond capital of Europe. One afternoon on our way to find the great diamond "deal," we came upon the house where Rembrandt painted many of his masterpieces. It had been turned into a museum. Indubitably, for a discovery just such as this, one enjoys living in Europe. No diamond was bought but several Rembrandts were seen for the first time and thoroughly enjoyed that afternoon. The entire city exuded an old world, graceful atmosphere.

As an artistic director, Jeanne Brabants behaved like a dictator. It was how she saw the running of a ballet company. She was on a history- making mission. Of me, she made much hullabaloo. She cast me in every principal role the company was rehearsing. The other dancers, so much more energetic than those I found in Stockholm, were being pushed aside. Of course there was jealousy. Word was that some of them had spoken with her about such casting. Though I could reap much from such circumstances, I was concerned about the big picture. I was not quite ready for her to be so enamored with American dancers, so much to the detriment of her other dancers. I was clearly the catalyst for discontent.

The highlight of the short time we spent there was working with John Butler, modern dance choreographer, on his ballet, "After Eden," based on the story of Adam and Eve. Though we did not perform this work until after we moved on from the company, it was one which we would dance often. Along with "Three Preludes," "After Eden" became a staple fare of our future guest engagements.

Performing with Ballet vanVlaanderen in sports halls around the country was gruesome work. I could not continue to dance four ballets a night, night after night. No dancer could perform such a grueling schedule. Jeanne Brabants referred to Nureyev when I told her she would have to better share the roles she gave to me. "Nureyev does it all the time!" I could not reason with her. She gave me an ultimatum which I rejected: I either dance as often as she wanted me to dance or I would leave the company. In January 1976, we left the company.

We immediately used our French connections and phoned the impresario, Youly Algaroff. He asked us to come to Paris. He had work for me and would find work for both of us in the interim.

Upon arrival in Paris, Algaroff contacted the dance critic for *Le Monde* newspaper and the photographer for *Danse Perspective* to meet with us. The interview was followed by a photo shoot. The European dance world was indeed fascinated with American dancers and Linda's reputation on the continent was already quite established. Paris received us well.

Youly had arranged a two week tour of Morocco during which I would dance with two former stars of the Paris Opera, Claire Motte and Claire Sombert, as guests with the Paris based Ballets Beranger. Prior to the tour, performances as guest artists with the Ballet de Opera du Nice in the French Riviera were also booked for Linda and me. There we would be joined by the then current *etoiles* (stars) of the Paris Opera, Noella Pontois and Cyril Anatassoff.

This six week period, from the time we left Belgium to the time we would leave France, gave us the opportunity to meet the elite of the French ballet world as well as experience a real flavor of the French capital. We met most of the dancers, including Nureyev, in Frano Franchetti's class which we attended daily. We were also introduced to the *croque monsieur* sandwich in the local café. Linda knew the meal as *jamon y queso* from her Spanish tours. This ham and cheese sandwich became a staple at lunch time; an integral part of the memories of Paris and Barcelona.

Having secured Youly's assistance, we began to map out a possible route to the future. Nureyev was starring in the London Festival Ballet's (LFB) production of "The Sleeping Beauty" at the *Palais de Sports*. A former Harkness dancer had recently joined the company. She had left for Europe immediately after the demise of the Harkness Company. We met her backstage following her afternoon rehearsal. She thought we should take company class the following day, which she arranged for us to do. Dame Beryl Grey was the company director at the time and she asked if we had something prepared to show her.

We danced the third act wedding *pas de deux* from "Beauty," thinking that would be appropriate. It went down well enough. Grey wanted to see more. "Three Preludes" was in the

LFB repertoire. Conveniently, the rehearsal pianist had the Rachmaninoff score in hand. Following our renderings, the company gave us a round of applause. Coming from one's peers, we found that very comforting. Grey signed both of us to Senior Artists contracts, one step below Principal Dancer status.

We celebrated that night with dinner at Maxim's, perhaps Paris' most famous restaurant. It is remembered for the tortoise shell dining room and the waiter who gave me my first lesson in tying a bow tie. There, in the restroom of the restaurant, he had rescued me from being able to get into the establishment at all. He also made me tie the tie three times before he was satisfied that he had done a proper job of teaching me. The taste of the food was surpassed only by the glowing feeling we had for our immediate future in London.

LFB administration had agreed that we honor our performance commitments to Algaroff. Linda would go on to London following the Opera du Nice performances and I would join her there following the Moroccan tour.

The February performances in the south of France were heaven sent. The area was all it had been touted to be and more. Walking around Nice, buying fresh, huge fruits at the market place, we settled at an outdoor café. On the wall of the café, directly above our table, was a very large poster announcing our performances. It was pretty impressive to see our names up there in such large print! The poster itself was a keeper, beautifully designed and distributed all over the town. The theatre manger had placed one of the posters on my dressing table before I got to the theatre. Years later, it was framed for display in our Dance Academy.

We danced Balanchine's Tchaikovsky "*Pas de Deux*" and the Act III pas *de deux* from "The Sleeping Beauty." Before leaving for Nice, I learned George Skibine's "Daphnis and Cloe" with Sombert and rehearsed "Le Corsair" with Motte.

The Road to London

Arriving in Rabat, Morocco, I met up with the Ballets Berenger at the hotel. We attended a meeting with officials of the French government who were sponsoring this first ever event: a professional dance tour of Morocco.

They explained to us that the audiences would be unusual in that many of them had never seen ballet or a dancer in a tutu. If this came off well, there would be other cultural events coming through the area. Ticket costs would be subsidized by the French government.

In Rabat we experienced our first samples of Moroccan cuisine: small dishes of exquisitely prepared vegetables in puree form, meats in exotic sauces, broiled pigeon and egg pastilla covered with powdered sugar, chocolate mousse in champagne and of course the main staple, couscous. The flavors were as wonderful as they were natural. As we traveled from town to town-Casablanca, Fez, Meknes, Agadir, Ouijda, Marrakech and Tangiers, we developed a keen taste for this food.

Having seen the movie "Lawrence of Arabia," I was prepared to recognize Peter O'Toole riding his white horse across the Sahara Desert, there in front of our rambling autobus! The riders we saw appeared frequently as we traveled the wide open desert space. They must have been coming from across the Atlas Mountain range. Their wild, flying white capes became an etched memory of the tour!

It was cold in the Desert. We stopped at villages that were set up in the middle of nowhere. Here, Nomads sold their wares of trinkets and fabrics and also goat's eyes from the animal they killed before our very eyes. They seemed to be living in the time of Christ! The rawness of the bare feet, usually a trait of the aged, fooled one who was looking at the faces before him. Both young and old were desert-worn by the winds as well as the management of life's necessities. These folks would not be seeing our performances.

The great culture of this kingdom in North Africa is largely represented in the dry goods, woolens, silks and jewelry that are displayed everywhere. The designs told the stories, the feel of the objects told the history. This history was relayed in the eyes and hands of the people who made these beautiful creations. Nowhere is this better exemplified than in the city of Fez. It was there that I felt the strongest sense of authentic Moroccan atmosphere.

The entire tour was sold out. We were expecting audiences who were totally inexperienced with live performance and who might behave accordingly. Instead, what we got were audiences who sat quietly mesmerized. At the final stop of the tour, Marrakech, we got a totally different response. There the audience rushed to the stage with gifts for us. We were quite unprepared for such overt appreciation. Several security guards calmed the mayhem, holding back the people and accepting the gifts for us. One gift I did accept from across the footlights. It was a silk robe (javala), black with gold edging. I realized such an experience would likely never happen again. I also realized that the sight of that city at night would also be a unique experience.

Horse drawn carriage taxis with tall gaslight candles on all four corners rushed through the town center shedding their light on the already golden buildings, reflecting the gold colored sand of the earth. There in the market square, snake charmers blew their flutes and musicians played and sang as the snakes came out to dance. Being able to walk, peruse and enjoy the foods while looking at such an abundance of beauty was like being on a movie set. This scene repeated every evening in Marrakech, Morocco.

Growing anxious to speak with Linda on the phone, I finally succeeded only to hear a very hoarse voice on the other end. As scheduled, she had flown onto London to begin rehearsal for the role of Kitri in LFB's production of "Don Quixote." She had developed a severe head cold that further developed into bronchitis. She hadn't been able to rehearse during the previous three days.

Anxious to be with her, I arrived in London in good time to take care of her. She was better soon; those wonderful eyes, that graceful personality! All was again right with the world. Though things were never really wrong, they were always very right when I was with her. I would take my time explaining the world I just left behind. I felt that the two weeks in Morocco were like a two month experience. Its cultural effect on me would take even more time to digest. Thus far, the Moroccan tour was at the extreme end of what traveling the world was all about.

London held the fascination for all the things we were basically familiar with and then some. Along with New York, this was a dancer's city. Apart from the commotion over getting a working visa for Linda, we couldn't be more at home. For a ballet director to bring a foreign ballerina to work in London was like bringing more caviar to Iran. Director Grey had her work cut out for her. However, within days she managed to secure Linda's legality for working and living in England.

Within weeks of my arrival in London, we began a tour of the provinces with LFB. Our initial performance with the company was as Kitri and Basilio in "Don Quixote." Things happened very quickly. In true British fashion, "we got on with it." The role of "Basilio," the barber, was great fun to perform. The ballet repertoire has roles defined by classical and demi-character (supporting roles defined by other than strict leading classical roles and choreography). Interestingly, this was one of the rare demi-character roles which required classical dancing choreography; hence, one had a lot more room for interpretation.

I learned a lot from watching my British colleagues tackle the part. They had the innate sense of wit that the role also required. Whether in the dressing rooms, at the canteen or at the local pub, the British humor, at large, is omnipresent. In the theatre setting, it appears to be wonderfully exaggerated. The Brits are all individual actors, really, and Basilio is, after all, an actor who likes to tease. The British dancers see the acting in a part as they are learning the steps.

We also danced Grey's production of "Swan Lake" on this tour, our debut scheduled for the city of Wolverhampton. This fine production placed greater emphasis on the role of Prince

Siegfried than others I had seen. Gray added choreography for the role of the Prince between Acts I and II and eliminated one intermission. It made good dramatic sense as did having two different ballerinas perform the roles of Odette (White Swan) and Odile (Black Swan). This was a "Swan Lake" that belonged to Prince Siegfried!

Upon arrival in Wolverhampton, we took a taxi to the hotel. I had both our salaries in cash in my bag. When we arrived at the theatre, I discovered that I had left the bag in the taxi. The following day was our debut. I received a note at the stage door. It was not the usual "good luck" greeting one might expect on the day of a debut. It was from the taxi driver's wife informing me that her husband had found my bag. She included her phone number. I called to arrange the retrieval.

As I arrived at the home a young boy, holding a news clipping announcing my debut as Prince Siegfried, opened the door. He was a local ballet student. I noticed my bag and the neatly sorted money on the dining room table; three hundred Pounds. When I remarked that the bag contained a greater sum, I was quickly told that three hundred pounds was all they found. I looked at the couple in silence. As I began to collect my belongings, the wife asked if I would be good enough to sign the news clipping for her son. "Dear Harold, may you grow up to be as honest as your parents are, sincerely…." After reading my writing, the couple cast a downward gaze. I handed them fifty pounds reward. They insisted that I not do that. "I would have nothing if you had not contacted me. I want you to have this," I replied. With that I returned to my waiting taxi and "got on with it!"

The "Swan Lake" debut was rewarding. The feeling of moving to that Tchaikovsky score in the warm glow of the blue stage lighting, adorned in finery was, in a way, very familiar to me. It didn't feel like a FIRST performance. I had been preparing a long time to become a prince of the Ballet. I was, however, overwhelmed to see Linda's entrance as Odette; similar to the way I felt seeing her walk up the aisle the day I married her. She was in her element.

On the other hand, I needed protection from the sight of my Argentine partner when she approached me as Odile one act later. Hers was a very fiery personality off stage. Onstage she was a whole lot hotter than your average tango dancer! These two very different dancers offered the right contrast for this ballet. Putting the interpretation together along with the execution of the dancing/partnering was the interesting part of this three hour long ballet. It was in such a manner that the classics always challenged the performer.

After the provincial tour, we had a three week season at the Coliseum in London. I was cast in two new works; as Prince Afron in the revival of "Le Coq d'Or,"and in "Rosamunda," a new ballet by former Royal Ballet dancer,

Ronald Hynd.

During the season, Algaroff called to asked Linda and me to dance in the French celebration of the American Bicentennial. The French wanted American composer, choreographer and dancers represented in a full evening Gala performance. "After Eden" would fit the bill perfectly. The performance was scheduled for July 4th in Nice. We were happy to oblige and to return to that beautiful area.

Daily, during rehearsal breaks at the London Coliseum, dancers would venture next door to the local "nafcaf" (small café) for tea, *etc*. Very possibly, two photos of us still hang in that little place. For certain, a photo of Margot Fonteyn in "Swan Lake" now hangs in my office.

Though small with only a few tables and chairs facing a counter for ordering amidst the mustiness of its atmosphere, the café was a popular dancer's hangout. England, and particularly London, was full of such places. After some time, the owners got to know the dancers. I think our being American intrigued them. They asked for a photo of us for them to put up on their wall.

There above the daily pot of boiling potatoes hung the loveliest photo of Fonteyn in "Swan Lake," wilting over the steam, unframed. "If you would trade me the Fonteyn photo, I will give you two of us?" I bargained. Gladly, she took Margot down and handed it to me. The following day I did as promised, all framed, and the day after that, there we were hanging up, steaming away in place of Fonteyn. It didn't seem entirely appropriate of course, but the proprietors were thrilled; a win-win for all, including Fonteyn.

It was at that "nafcaf" where we would assess our positions and futures with LFB. Having been inside the company for six months, we saw how things worked there. We saw that the casting for London suddenly had guest artists names in place of those who had done the roles on tour. Nureyev aside, did box office need guest dancers to make the budget? We realized we would have mostly demi-soloist roles to perform behind the guest dancers in London and other major cities and would have to wait a long time for our "principal" turn to come around. At thirty- one and thirty, it was a real issue for us. How long could we wait? Were we about five years late? Five years late is very late in the ballet business.

A 'Beauty' in Beautiful South Africa

The director of BALLET INTERNATIONAL (BI) was contracting for Principal dancers. We had made his short list. The new company was the buzz around the London dance scene. Larry Long, the director-designate, was not known in England but had an extensive reputation in the States. Ben Stevenson, who was very well known in England, was signed to choreograph his versions of two full- length ballets for the company and the country of South Africa would be financing the entire venture.

The venture was the brainchild of Max Martin, a British

businessman married to a soloist of the Royal Ballet. The story goes that one evening while having dinner in the company of Fonteyn and Nureyev, Martin got the idea to become an Impresario. Some months earlier he had presented a group called "Stars of the Ballet" on a tour throughout South Africa. He then arranged a sponsorship by South Africa to have its own international ballet company. Hence, BI was born.

For those contracted as the principal dancers of BI an important need would be met: opportunities to dance often. We decided to accept Long's invitation to dinner. His sincerity and honesty were worn on his sleeve. We both liked him and felt an immediate trust with him. He was excited by the prospects of the company and happy to report that the offer was all it portended to be. Along with four other principal couples, we would be dancing and touring a lot. We decided to join Ballet International.

The timing couldn't have been better. LFB was on an extended break. We made an appointment to speak with Grey. She did not make any significant offer that would change our minds about leaving LFB. The contract she did offer us was the same contract we were on: no promotion to Principal status, no principal role performance dates. We explained that she was helping us to move over to BI. It was clear that her needs and those of BI were like day and night.

Stevenson set and rehearsed his productions of "The

Sleeping Beauty" and "The Nutcracker" on BI during the summer of 1976. Three other ballets were choreographed to complete a triple bill. The three month tour of South Africa was to begin in September and go through mid December. Auditions had produced a full regiment of soloists and corps de ballet. New costumes and sets were designed and built in London. By late August, we looked like a full fledged ballet company.

Eighteen hours after leaving Heathrow Airport in London, the company arrived in Wellcome, South Africa. With an altitude similar to Mexico City and after so long a trip, most of us felt light headed. Looking around, I noticed that Linda was missing. One of the *corps* members alerted me to the fact that she seemed to have fainted while waiting at the luggage carousel. While one of the dancers alerted the authorities that we needed a doctor, I picked her up and carried her to the nearest seats. She was quickly brought around through the efforts of a nurse who administered smelling salts to her. Though she seemed well enough for a scheduled interview with the Johannesburg Press, I began to answer for both of us.

"What's it like spending twenty four hours a day with the same person every day?" "Did both of you always want to dance professionally?" and on and on. Soon Linda seemed able to speak for herself. A few questions later and the interview was cut short in lieu of the inoculations that we were expecting to take before leaving the airport. We laughed the following day when we saw the interview in print. It was on the cover of the Sunday Magazine section, accompanied by a photo of us looking like we did not like being together ANYTIME of the day! The writer made up the rest of the story about us. It wasn't a bad read given that we said very little of it. Welcome to Wellcome, South Africa!

On our first free day we were taken to a diamond mine. It was a Sunday, the day that the miners celebrate with dancing in their Wellington boots to the rhythms of African drums. Hundreds of men in deep knee bends swaying side to side and to and fro to the beat made their way into the large stadium next to the mine. Children and other adults from various parishes danced as well. There was also a choir of young boys singing in the typical South African "clicking" mode. The entire scene resembled a rehearsed performance, not the regular Sunday offering that it was. We had just been baptized with South African atmosphere!

These were happy, smiling people. Given the Apartheid conditions at that time, I was perplexed by this happiness. Seeing their human spirit overcoming obstacles would, time and again, open my mind to these people and their country.

South Africa's population consisted of sixteen million blacks and four million whites. That the whites were in power was one incredible fact of life in this most beautiful of countries. The other equally incredible fact was the reverence the black man had for his white master, even though he could not use the urinal he cleaned at the airport.

We traveled the breath of the country: From Wellcome to Pretoria, from Johannesburg to Bloemfontaine, from St. Pietersmaritsburg to Port Elizabeth, from Capetown to Durban. The BI company, repertoire and dancers were well received. The Afrikaners were getting to know us. We were getting to know our supporters, PACOFS (Performing Arts Council for Orange Free State). I wondered if we were what they had in mind. They were sold a package that was very different from the guest stars of various world wide companies that they had been originally smitten with. My thoughts were pacified in that this was a company they could call their own, with stars from various world wide companies. That seemed like something to hold onto. Guest stars are just that; they are guests.

We made our debut together in "The Sleeping Beauty," performed in Capetown at the Nico Milan Theater. Capetown boasted a mountain in the middle of the city! On a night when the fog came in from the Indian Ocean one could look up and see a table cloth formed by the fog, gracefully hanging over the flat topped, appropriately named Table Mountain; imagine a mountain in the middle of Lincoln Center in New York City! The Nico Milan was indeed Capetown's Lincoln Center. A new Opera House, it was state of the art in every way.

Dress rehearsal went extremely well for us. Linda, dancing the role of "Aurora," was in great form. I had easily imagined her in the role. Having rehearsed and developed the ballet together was the wonderful part. I had long realized that if a professional dancer doesn't like rehearsing he probably should do something else. Generally, the performances are few and far between the rehearsals.

Minutes before the dressers handed Linda the fresh rose petals she would throw out onto the stage as she made her entrance, I found her way too busy in the rosin box. Usually, if at all, she would place just the tips of her pointe shoes into the box once or twice just to get them slightly rosined. Now she couldn't get enough rosin on the toes of her shoes! I went over to hug her, knowing that she was nervous. I wasn't used to seeing her show her nervousness. The roses in hand, she looked at me a little like a doe facing a light beam and said, "Well, if I am not ready now, I never will be!"

To those famous strains of Tchaikovsky, she ran through the arbor ways of the first act set, throwing the petals. The music had taken her. She was on her way!

Chills ran through my body as I heard the audience response to the finish of her first variation. I let out my breath for her. Thoughts of her Italian heritage came to mind as I watched her honorable intent and thorough integrity as she approached the famous "Rose Adagio," so innate was her approach. She was everything Tchaikovsky wrote for, everyone's accepted Aurora. I couldn't wait to get out there with her!

The performance was a wish come true. Suddenly, the Joffrey ballet seemed a long, long time ago. This was more than just adding another "prince" role to my repertoire. It was also about developing the careers together. That evening was one of those 'special' events few dancers ever experience. As it happened to be my birthday the following day, we decided to celebrate with a drive seventy miles west to the Cape of Good Hope.

This was a spectacular ride, comparable in some ways to the Rt. 1 "Big Sur" drive from San Francisco to Los Angeles. The biggest difference was the flora; here we had Protea (South Africa's native flower) instead of dandelion growing along the edges of the road being overlooked by purple jacaranda trees under the brilliant blue sky of South Africa.

Stopping for breakfast, we picked up a copy of the local newspaper, "The Capetown Gazette," and saw the front page news. No, it was not about our debut the previous night. It was all about Jimmy Carter, the peanut farmer from Plains, Georgia, who had just been elected President of the United States. All of that seemed particularly far away that day. We imagined the happiness other Americans must have been feeling about the new president. For the moment, we had a rendezvous with another part of history; the spot where Vasco de Gama anchored his ship hundreds of years ago.

One could not actually get down to Cape Point. The view

from the top was of jutting stones resembling sharp knife points, the results of centuries of erosion. Any attempt at descending would be an act of suicide. Still, overlooking where the Indian and Atlantic Oceans converge was a spectacular sight. The day was perfect!

Several pages on, The Gazette dance critic did not write of our "perfect" debut as Aurora and Prince Florimund but he did write of Linda's natural way with the role and my caring partnering and impressive *cabrioles* (jumps where legs meet then open in the air)! We would have to do what everyone else always did, after all; practice to be perfect! We'd show them "perfection" in England!

As we entered the second month of the tour our stagehands, who were direct descendants of the original Bushmen, could often be found trying out some of the dance steps on stage between matinee and evening shows. Walking into the backstage area before my evening performance one late afternoon, I saw one of the stagehands giving a decent effort at attempting one of my variations. He even got the spacing right. I was his only audience so I applauded loudly. Then to my surprise, his colleagues appeared from the darkness of stage left to join my clapping and insisted on showing their "stuff" too. Certainly, at that moment, my theory that all humans are basically dancers was reconfirmed: first man moved, his heart beat giving him his rhythm. Through the ages, some men only know such inner feelings, some go on to study dancing, and some even make a living working as a dancer and some become a prince of the ballet! All, I believe, are naturally connected to dancing.

While on our next stop in Port Elizabeth I learned of the shocking news that PACOF's was rescinding future support from BI. I was having breakfast alone and read the news in a local paper. The government officials were alarmed to find out that Max Martin was not paying the bills, that embezzlement was suspected. South African Airlines had not been paid. The costume and point shoe bills were outstanding. The airline alerted PACOFS. Where was the money going?

Over the next few days, I also learned that several of the stars who were having their salaries wired to various European banks had learned that the accounts had not received monies from BI. Max had been diverting the money. Max was a criminal!

On the flight to Durban, I told Linda about what I had read. I handed her the news article. At that time, we were among the few to know. We decided to confront our directors. Finding the appropriate time and circumstance to do it was our top priority.

We opened the Durban performances with "Beauty." I was still awaiting my new second act costume at curtain time. Gillian, our costume mistress, assured me it would be ready in time. Everyone was sweating profusely. Durban, at that time of the year is one hundred percent humid. The Indian Ocean was nearly eighty degrees. Onstage we felt like we were in the Indian Ocean.

Gillian arrived in the wings with the new blue tunic, elaborately studded with stones and appliqués, just five minutes before my entrance. I changed into it and, though it did not feel well fitted, I had little time to discuss the matter. It could be addressed later.

During the vision scene, while lowering Linda from an overhead lift, I felt the front of the tunic pull. It did not open. When I came offstage, I spoke with Gillian. She knew it needed more work. After the curtain calls, I walked Linda to her dressing room. While she was undressing I noticed a straight pin plugged almost completely into her left thigh. We looked at each other. We realized it had been there from the second act *pas de deux,* an hour earlier. She had changed tights between Acts II & III without disturbing or noticing the pin. We had to laugh at the level of concentration this ballet took from her!

This was a most extreme example of what generally happens when adrenaline is working during a performance. Several years earlier, while dancing my variation from "The River" with ABT in Los Angeles, an earthquake occurred! People got up and left the theatre. I thought that my dancing must be leaving a lot to be desired! When I went into the wings, the others dancers said, "Did you feel that, the shaking?" I felt nothing.

That night while my roommate and I were in our room, we not only felt another quake but we saw the pictures on the walls moving; the adrenaline no longer being enhanced by performance.

With the following two days free, we took the opportunity to rent a car and drive six hours north to the Hluhluwe Game Reserve. We wanted to get far away from what was going on in the company, far enough away to think and talk about it. The reserve would be a perfect setting. Visiting a reserve was something I had actually dreamed about doing. In my dream the animals came up to the car, close enough to be fed by hand.

As we entered the reserve, the baboons were the first to announce themselves, jumping right up on the hood of the car. Then the rhinoceros approached my side of the car. I felt the nature everywhere; total NATURE! Though we had been told not to get out of the car let alone feed the animals, I wanted to. Linda held me back. We gradually moved on to the wildebeest, springbok and elephants. The silence of the place was deafening. We spent the whole afternoon INSIDE the car! I never knew if they would eat from my hand. I was freed only when we were again outside the reserve's gates. There, outside the gates, were the Masai Tribes people. We spent time admiring them and their work with wooden bowls and trinkets before beginning the drive back to Durban.

Max met us at the stage door, asking that we dance the

matinee and evening performances the following day. The alternating cast had walked out over an undisclosed dispute. It turned out to be about their salaries. I asked him for our salaries. We had received ours in cash the entire tour. He said they would be late; all salaries would be late that week. I told him that we would not dance either show if the money wasn't in hand by the half- hour call. We asked him to explain the news article that we showed to him. Larry walked in on the conversation. Neither of them was forthcoming with an explanation. We left for the hotel and dinner with Andre Presser, our conductor. What did he know? What did Larry know?

The following day we were paid in cash and danced both performances. Max called a full company meeting between shows to explain that costs were beyond the planned budget and that he had to borrow money to complete the tour. He said he was requesting the British government provide funds for the upcoming British tour. He did his level best to make us feel that things would be all right.

We were in the midst of the British tour when the government announced that it had denied the funding request. We were facing the demise of a ballet company for the second time in our careers.

The final performance in Coventry was preceded by performances in Bournemouth, Newcastle, Hull, Paignton, Liverpool, Blackpool, Oxford and Bath. At the Bath performance Yvonne, my partner in one of the triple bill ballets, was missing. The word was that she had gone off with Max. They had been seeing each other on the tour. Gone off? When the dust settled it was reported that the two of them along with the missing money were some where in the Isle of Skye, Scotland.

Apart for the balance of our contracts which would have taken us through the month of June, we had received every penny that we earned. Still, we were four months short of expected earnings. We either spent the next period litigating for the balance or getting on with our careers. A general counsel convened on behalf of all the dancers; barristers were assigned and each dancer's contact information was given.

The flat we owned in Lexham Gardens, bought before the South African tour, was a comforting sight when we returned to London. The area was lovely and very conveniently located in the section of Knightsbridge. Our New York apartment had been sublet during these two years. The contract on that was nearly up. We considered returning to the States.

Three days after our return to London from Coventry, a call came from Boris Trailine. Though he was running neck and neck with Algaroff as THE European agent to be associated with, Algaroff kindly referred us to him for his new proposals. Firstly, Club Mediterranean in Marbella, Spain wanted a *pas de deux* to be danced along with their scheduled entertainment. They would fly us round trip from London and give us a week at the club for one ten minute performance. Trailine thought it would also serve as somewhat of a rest for us. We accepted, we danced and we rested. It was memorable for the performance but also for riding the horses in the nearby mountains and for visiting the Alhambra in Granada. The view from our room faced the Rock of Gibraltar and beyond that was the city of Tangiers, the northern most tip of Morocco. I remembered it well.

We returned to Granada some weeks later as guest artists with Le Grand Ballet du Geneve where we danced in the outdoor Generalife Gardens. Thereafter, Trailine arranged for us to meet the director of Ballet du Wallonie, in Charleroi, Belgium. The company was in need of a principal couple. It was a typically European company in an atypically ugly city. This was the home of pomme frites drowning in mayonnaise and Stella Artois beer finished off with Gauloise cigarettes. The entire place smelled of a brewery and the sky looked as one might imagine the aftermath of a nuclear explosion; orange everyday. This was an industrial town.

Alicia Alonso's "Swan Lake" and a premiere of Attilio Labis' "Spartacus" were the main productions scheduled for the season. The later sounded to be the more interesting of the two. The setting was 1968 Paris, during the student uprising. The former would offer Linda the opportunity of dancing both Odette and Odile roles. We decided to take the positions though the end of the Charleroi season, giving us time to reassess our new circumstances.

Touring throughout Germany began before we had time to settle in Charleroi. Again, the main benefit for us was the opportunity to dance often. The experience of dancing "Spartacus" was unlike any other. It involved fighting and other war techniques woven into the choreography. This helped keep the focus on him as a warrior away at war. It worked particularly well during the *pas de deux* with Virgie (his wife) which was depicted as though he was absent (she imagines him there during the dance). After learning of the death of Spartacus, Virgie has the final scene of the ballet accompanied by her small son by Spartacus. She stands in the middle of the stage. Beside her is the son dressed in the warrior uniform of his father. The final spot light focuses on the boy raising his little sword. Fadeout!

We returned to Charleroi for the season there but first, a surprise: Ella Fitzgerald was scheduled to give one performance with The Tommy Flanagan Trio on our stage the night before the ballet opened.

"Robert, you know Ms. Fitzgerald has severe sight problems, would you mind if she uses your dressing room tonight, yours being the closest to the stage?" asked the theatre manager. "I'd be honored to do that for Ms. Fitzgerald," I responded. "Would you be so kind as to have two tickets set aside for me?" I asked. My circumstances were completely different now, thirteen years after I first served Miss Ella a meal. However, I still recalled the order and knew I had a chance of surprising her. Would she remember me?

Ten minutes before the show, I knocked on my dressing room door. "Medium rare with raw onion, lettuce, no tomato but with LOTS of ketchup," I announced. Miss Ella quickly opened the door, "Miss Ella it's Bobby, your waiter from the Americana Hotel." Shaking that white hanky, she smiled, "What are you doing here?" "I dance here Miss Ella, you are using my dressing room and my wife and I are coming to hear you sing again tonight," I answered. After a hug, she backed up a bit and smiled, "I told you to keep working at it, didn't I? I told you, you would make it, Bobby!"

With Mr. Flanagan assistance, Miss Ella made her way onto the stage:

"Oh the sharks bite with their teeth, babe, Love for Sale, Advertising young love for sale, You'd be so easy to love...."
And there, again, Ella Fitzgerald flew us all to the moon.

Hiatus

We were very happy to be back in New York, back in our apartment. It was a time to reflect, see friends, and catch up with our families. It was like a big present all rolled into one. We were signed with a New York agent who scheduled us for performances in Upstate New York, Maryland, Long Island and a brief two week return to Johannesburg, South Africa with "Stars of American Ballet." These dates were spread throughout the coming year, giving us time in between. We were back in classes with former teachers, having friends from various ballet companies over to dinner, traveling to see families and enjoying Manhattan. The year was 1978.

My siblings had, in the fifteen years since I first left for New York, developed their own lives. Only Mother seemed stuck in time. Though the circumstances surrounding her life were certainly difficult, it became all too clear that one can also learn what not to do from one's parent's example. She would get lonelier as all the children found their lives, mates and careers.

We had time for a trip home to see each family. We felt the love of our families. We tried to return that love while providing perspective to each other. As we looked at our lives through their eyes, we realized how proud they were. The work we did and the way we lived was very different from them but the majority was not judgmental. It was clear that they knew one day we would no longer travel so frequently, that our work would change and that we would one day raise a family, just like most of them were doing.

I took advantage of the time I had to begin to think about teaching. I took offers to teach as they came along. First, at Ballet Arts in Carnegie Hall, one class a week, then two classes a week at New York Theatre Workshop, then three classes at Steps Studio, *etc.* I worked with Elena Tchernichova again as often as possible. I liked the expression of teaching, the act of transferring information. The class attendees seemed to like me and my classes. Due to rehearsal schedule, I wasn't able to be totally consistent with the teaching commitment but I was exhilarated by liking it so much. Instinctively, I knew that the dancing part of my career was the very best part. Still, life after dancing might just be okay after all.

We were preparing "Three Preludes" for the Poughkeepsie Ballet Theatre Fundraising Gala in Upstate New York when Sallie Wilson, ABT's renowned dramatic ballerina, asked me to partner her in her new ballet set to the music of Schuman. She was premièring the work at the same Gala. I was glad to have the chance to work with her as her pure sense for movement and drama had always fascinated me. The gala was very successful financially with all monies going to the Poughkeepsie Ballet Theatre. I have often remembered that performance for being our very best dancing of "Three Preludes." Perhaps that was the result of performing gratis. Were we under less pressure?

For two weeks during the spring we experienced the joy of returning to and being remembered in South Africa. For this visit we added "La Bayadere" to our repertoire. The critics were especially happy to see us again. The political situation there, however, remained unchanged.

From there we left the Stars of American Ballet and flew to Tehran, Iran to be the guest artists for the first Iranian International Ballet Festival. This was also our second trip to Teheran, the first being on that extraordinary European tour with Harkness Ballet in 1974.

This trip had been arranged by one of Linda's former partners at Harkness Ballet, Ali Pourfarrokh. He was then the director of the Iranian National Ballet. We danced opening night then had the following three days free. We were flown to Ramsar near the Caspian Sea for sightseeing. This simple fishing village is the area where the caviar is taken from the sturgeon, the roses are purple and minks roam Mink Mountain. Before returning to Tehran for the middle performances of the run, we bought a pound of "gold" caviar to bring to our friends in Geneva. This was the caviar the Shah of Iran ate; no black caviar for him! After several more appearances, we ended our engagement by dancing with the entire company at the final performance of the Festival.

The following morning I went to the Grand Bazaar to buy jewelry. There I noticed much tension in the streets. Fires were burning and trucks were stopping to randomly pick up pedestrians. I was told to leave the city as soon as I could. For the first time in anyone's memory, the Grand Bazaar was closed. The people were uprising.

Politically, the Shah was out of favor. As had happened to the Pavlavi family previously, the Shah was being deposed. For years, he had been moving his people too quickly into the mainstream of westernization. Now his efforts were backfiring on him and his family. It was a repeat of history for the Iranian people.

Back inside the hotel, I explained to Linda what I thought was going on in the city. She was watching the news on television and was aware of the danger at hand. We left seven hours early for our flight to Geneva, gold caviar in hand. The date was May 29, 1979. The Shah and his family flew out of Tehran to Egypt on the flight before ours. The Iranian government was in the hands of the people.

Our plane made a brief stop in Rome and then went on to Geneva. Upon arrival I asked the stewardess to retrieve the caviar for me. She came back empty handed. Apologizing, she explained that the flight's refrigerator containers had been switched in Rome. The caviar was in a refrigerator in the Rome airport! I asked her to find me another pound of "gold" caviar, perhaps from the first class kitchen. She claimed there was no "gold" caviar on board. I decided to hold my ground, much to Linda's chagrin. I stated that I would not get off of the plane without the caviar. Indeed, I was the only one left some ten minutes after everyone else, including Linda, had disembarked.

Down the isle the stewardess came, "gold" caviar in hand. She had it brought over from another Iran Air airplane, also on the tarmac at the same time; a full pounds' worth! I had my present for our friends. Again I learned that perseverance is almost always worth the effort.

Before returning to New York, we took the opportunity to meet Linda's Great aunts and their families in Florence, Italy.

Italy was the seat of great art, opera, architecture, food, wine and style. It was an intensely stimulating country. Florence would have been enough on its own, but meeting and spending time with Linda's loving family made it especially memorable. The time spent in Verona on the ABT tour in 1970 was very good preparation for this visit.

We had been fortunate enough to see many other parts of the world yet Italy was not on any of our ballet tours. And so we got the chance to enjoy it without working, to feel the warmth of these beautiful people whose natural speaking voices sounded like bel canto (singing). Leaving Florence, one had a greater sense of all that the Italians had wrought for the world at large to admire. I fell in love all over again.

When we returned to New York, Heinz Spoerli, the director of the Basel Ballet in Switzerland, was in the city and contacted Linda about joining his company. He had sent her a note backstage during our LFB Coliseum season in 1976. In the note he wrote of his admiration for her, that she was his perfect "Juliet." At this time, Linda felt that it would be good to be in a company again. She was not smitten with guest performances. The director's proposal was flattering. I was more interested in developing a teaching technique than dancing in a company again. Spoerli offered me the position of Assistant Ballet Master. We were grateful for his agreeing to what we both wanted. It meant not only living in Switzerland but also being able to visit Connie Anderson in Gstaad any given weekend. That was luxury!

Having plenty of time before our plane departed, we decided to go to LaGuardia Airport from JFK for dinner. We knew of a very good restaurant there. On the way back to JFK, the taxi became ensnarled in a major traffic jam. We were stuck in that jam for just a little too long. Upon arriving at JFK, we ran to the departure gate. It had just closed. They would not reopen it. The flight took off without us. That was the first and last time we have ever missed a flight.

Several hours later, we were on a flight to Zurich, Switzerland with an eight hour layover in Frankfurt, Germany on our way to Basel. It was not a good beginning.

Plans for Linda in Basel included an original production of "The Nutcracker." More appetizing would be the stage production of Spoerli's "Traume" (Dream), created for German television the previous year with the Stuttgart Ballet. It's the story of Mathilde Wiesendonk, wife of the famed Swiss Industrialist Otto Wiesendonk, and her love affair with composer Richard Wagner. It is danced to Wagner's not so well known "Wiesendonk Lieder," which was written for Mathilde. Linda's success in this ballet was predictable. From her days in the Boston Ballet where she had much praise for her portrayal of "Le Combat" to her interpretation of "Eaters of Darkness" on film with the Harkness Ballet, dance acting was her forte.

The Swiss, German and French critics were unanimous: "Basel Ballet now has a world class ballerina!" I was feeling my way teaching company class and rehearsing ballets beside the well known ballet master, Peter Apple. Though it was a fruitful period for me, it was one that would satiate Linda to the extent that she began to talk seriously about wanting to settle and start a family.

While we were in Basel for the year's contract, we did visit with Connie Anderson in Gstaad often, once working with her on "Three Preludes" for which she accompanied us on her grand piano right there in the former Harkness Ballet studio, now turned into her chalet home. There were all of thirty-five people in the audience. This remains our most charming experience before an audience and our most intimate!

At the end of the contract we realized that it was time to seriously consider our long term future. It would necessarily include moving out of New York and beginning a family. If we wanted to start our own school, it would be best for us to do it while we were young enough to establish it.

A final journey, after our European work was done, took us to the north of Italy to visit Venice, Murano and Burano before returning to New York to "get on with it". This was a fitting trip, full of the many wonders of that part of the country and a time for looking back at that first meeting with Jeanne Brabants whose initial contract offer was instrumental in getting us started in Europe. More appropriately, one should thank Rebekah Harkness who, by closing her company when she did, once again made possible for us a career, with still more travel, that we could ever have imagined! Those Venetian meals were some of the best we have ever had together. I can't help but think that it was, in large part, because of the conversations and memories we had to share.

Getting on With It

How do dancers really feel about quitting? Dancers wind down, generally. The feelings run the gamut of ranges depending on how one felt the career developed and whether or not one had enough time on the stage. The latter is very important; the former is open to debate. One can now look to other long awaited interests.

Why do dancers often dance past their prime? Firstly, they love what they do and do not want to stop. Secondly, they fear what lies ahead, even though they knew all along that retirement time was coming earlier for them than for the rest of the working population. Many are concerned with the cultural change they will experience by leaving the confines of a major city for the unfamiliar open spaces and lifestyle of the suburbs where their futures (as teachers, directors, choreographers) often lay. Time easily passes by.

Our New York agents were in contact with many of the regional board of directors throughout the country. We asked them to let us know of an opening for company directors, especially in the Virginia area. During our individual states' tours, we both had fond memories of that state. It bordered the north and the south, was not so far from Washington, DC and offered great beauty of landscape and, of course, the ocean.

After our final return from Europe, Linda took on a teaching position with Eliot Feld's New Ballet School in Manhattan. I resumed teaching here and there around the city. As always, we took class. We were in transition.

Within weeks, our agent called to tell us of an opening in Newport News, Virginia. The Virginia State Ballet was meeting with potential directors for their company and school. We would receive clarifying information at our meeting the following day when we had an appointment with our agent to sign contracts as guest teachers for the North Carolina School of the Arts summer dance program.

The possibility in Virginia looked very interesting, everything in fact that one would look for. If one wanted to venture out into the tricky world of directing an arts organization in America, run by a Board of Directors, this sounded better than most. One can only imagine himself in that atmosphere and hope that he could make a difference. We knew the stories, the nightmares of what can happen when one is dependent on the fundraising of board members. ABT, New York City Ballet and Joffrey were prime examples. We were all raised with the struggle of fundraising for the arts in the USA.

Owing to prior commitments, we would not be able to meet with the board in Virginia until the end of August and, at that, would not be able to begin there before October first. That agreed to, we began to think in terms of leaving Manhattan permanently. Like others before us, we needed time to adjust to what looked to be a very different kind of future.

While teaching the intermediate ballet class at Steps Studio on 55th St., I noticed an inquiring face peeking through the doorway. It was the second time I saw Mike watching the class. The third time, I asked him to come in. Watching him move, I recognized a spiritual purity in his dancing. His name was Mike Myers. He was from Boston, a former wrestler who took up dancing following a visit to his sister's dance class. What he lacked in stature and physical gifts, he more than made up for by the honesty of his masculine movement qualities.

I took to him right away, knowing I could help him develop properly. As it turned out, he was looking for a new mentor and was serious about a dance career. His buddy, Jake, was a trained dancer who had stopped. Mike was set on getting Jake to resume dancing. They were working as handymen, refurbishing brownstones on the upper west side. They began to show up consistently in my class. They were both nineteen years old. Mike decided to apply for a scholarship at the summer program in North Carolina. Jake was not so sure. Mike was accepted on full scholarship and joined us for the summer.

Intensive training during the summer solidified Mike's resolve to work with us toward his goal. He was prepared to follow us to Virginia. First, we had to get there. We flew to Norfolk at the end of the summer session. The board members seemed typical in their roles. They were friendly and very interested in our plans for the company and school. We planned on bringing dancers from New York to the company in Virginia and to oversee the three schools there which were part of the organization. It was a mighty task but we both thought it was a good place for us to begin. We agreed on a contract and salary.

Jake returned to class and announced that he, too, would be joining us in Virginia. Both Jake and Mike wanted to become members of the Virginia State Ballet company.

A mere six months into the venture the board went belly up; the 'nightmare' rearing its ugly head AGAIN! I can say that it is never really foreseeable. In circumstances such as these, where a group of people put their minds and checkbooks together, the very act itself is somewhat of a miracle when it does develop successfully. It was particularly true during that time when many such efforts just did not make headway. The demands of the commitment are often too difficult. And so it was with this particular board of directors. There was little history of professional ballet in Virginia. We had hoped to make a difference.

During this time, I choreographed three ballets and Linda set the ballet, "*Pas de Quatre.*" We gave performances throughout the area. There was much good feeling for what we, as artistic directors, were doing. Our students and their parents wanted very much for us to stay in the area. We could do that or we could try another board in another area. Clearly, we wanted to bring what we knew to those who were the future dancers and audiences and, thereby, provide a future for ourselves. There was a lot of goodwill in Newport News, Virginia. That and the student's tuition was what we would have to restart with.

A long weekend at North Carolina's Outer banks helped us clear our heads and decide to stay in the area. We would open our own academy and we would develop what we were brought there to develop.

The Dance Academy

Initially our academy held classes in a former modeling agency. It was near by and had mirrors and *barres* already in place. It was obviously once a ballet studio! We conducted classes there while the six thousand square foot Chinese laundry we had located and were in the process of converting into a proper dance academy was being prepared for us. Above the space was a four bedroom apartment. It had been a great find for us.

After contracting for the bulk of the reconstruction, Mike and Jake put their renovation skills to use by proudly building the tongue and groove, basket weave flooring. Students and their parents helped wherever they could. The Dance Academy opened on schedule, September 7, 1982.

By October the local chapter of the American Association of University Women (AAUW) offered to sponsor our first performance: an adaptation of "The Sleeping Beauty" in which Linda and I led the academy students. This successfully received first effort paved the way for our ultimate venture, Ballet Virginia. Importantly, we were benefiting from the merits of our first six months work in the area.

At this time, the subject of starting a family was revisited. We were, comparatively speaking, settled. We began to discuss the possibility of adoption. It had always been in our conversations regarding parenthood. During our travels, we saw many children who were improperly cared for. In the Dominican Republic, various parts of India and on the Middle Eastern continent we saw the greatest number of such unfortunate children. If we imagined that even in developed countries there is a great need to adopt infants before they fall into the foster care programs, then becoming adoptive parents seemed an important role that we could take on in society. With the option to become pregnant open for many years without results, perhaps the message was ours for the taking. We spoke with agencies in our area and made applications. What we did not factor in was the lack of newborns due to the high abortion rate. Still, the process was in motion and, more importantly, we were sure of wanting to see it through.

A local distraction to the adoption process was the In-Vitro clinic across the bay in Norfolk, Va. At the time it was the largest clinic of its kind in the country. In little time, we realized that we did not want to play "the hand of God" in this matter. We ruled out using the In-Vitro process for the purpose of creating a family.

With the Academy's opening day well behind us, we began to add teachers and classes to our curriculum. As co-directors, Linda and I taught the majority of the classes and oversaw the others. It was a different type of experience than what we expected to be having. It was our own business. Our task was before us; to develop our teaching methods and the young students who were in our charge.

It was clear from the onset that Linda would be relying on her Cecchetti (England's Royal Academy of Dancing) background while I worked my knowledge of the Vaganova system. The resulting product would land somewhere in between which we felt was appropriate for the American dancer. We arranged to have guest teachers from New York to work in our Summer School and to have masters of other forms work with the students, specifically a Martha Graham dancer to introduce modern technique as well as a Jazz teacher to take charge of the that technique.

We held student demonstrations at the end of the year. This, in lieu of annual recitals for the youngest students, sufficed well. Once they were sufficiently developed, they performed in the annual productions with the older students.

"The Sleeping Beauty' adaptation gave way to a full production of "A Midsummer Night's Dream." We alternated these two works during the first years while adding new, shorter ballets for outreach performances. At this time, Jake auditioned for and was accepted to the Connecticut Ballet. Michael, now like a son to us, remained to develop further. By 1985, we set plans in motion for the professional company we originally planned to direct in the area. It had been five years since our arrival. Our reputations and credentials were established. The product was successful. In the fall we encouraged Mike to audition in the larger dance world. He succeeded in signing a contract with the Oakland Ballet. His sudden absence was felt by one and all.

It was then that we were told by the adoption agencies that our incomes did not qualify for a new born child. With so many couples having been accepted as potential adoptive parents, the one fair criterion would be income level. We weren't even in contention. We decided to remove our name from the adoption list, allowing others who were financially qualified to move up a notch in the process. Having informed family and friends of our adoption intentions, we decided to leave the subject of parenting in the hands of fate.

Only days after our decision, my brother-in-law called with the news of a possible adoption. My younger sister, Diane, had identified a birth mother. Were we still interested? In retrospect I feel that if an adoption was going to be identified for us, it would happen in such a private way, just like that.

Given my sister's extraordinarily helpful nature, this news was as exciting for her as it was for us. Whenever I reminisce about it I still can only imagine the exceptional feeling of doing that much for another person.

Our son, Matthew Robert Brassel, was born two weeks late. He was considerate enough to wait until his professional parents were freed from their summer course commitment. He arrived the day after our session closed!

Leaving the Academy the morning of his birth, I remembered that I had forgotten to leave food for our German shepherd, Beauty. Linda was already in the car. The phone rang as I was returning to her. I thought to not answer it but changed my mind. "You have a son!" said my sister Diane. I next remember that Linda walked into the academy's office. Her large eyes met mine. I nodded yes. We shared a long embrace. The soundness of this process rang loud and clear. We felt that we three were meant to be together; that each of us was now more than we were before. Though I had never had such a feeling in my life, I knew it would be counted as the best there was, right up there with being alive.

If one had a choice, one would have an academy full of dance students when one's baby arrives. We were supplied with diapers for a year and never looked far for a sitter. Everyone wanted to see the baby, all the time. He was a wonderful distraction for the students and parents. Nonetheless, one needed to maintain some semblance of order: NO MORE BEING LATE TO CLASS BECAUSE YOU WERE HOLDING MATTHEW!

The Ballet Guild, comprised mostly of parents with vested interests, was developed to oversee the workings of the performances. This developed into the Board of Directors for the professional company, Ballet Virginia. We retained ownership of the academy. We held auditions in Manhattan as well as throughout the local area. The first season's program would have two of my works, Bizet's "Symphony in C" and Gershwin's "Rhapsody in Blue" along with "Three Preludes" and a dramatic ballet, "A Lover's Tale" from the National Ballet of Canada choreographed by the Belgian choreographer, Marc Bogaerts. Marc's was a very nice presence to be in. He brought the European sensibility back to us and that style to the company. Bill Como, Editor-in-Chief of DANCE MAGAZINE agreed to be master of ceremonies for the debut of the company in Norfolk, Virginia the following March.

The critics politely praised this first showing of the professional company but indicated that they eagerly awaited further developments. That indicated to me that it was a cautious debut.

This was no longer an outgrowth of a local dance academy. These were professionals and now the Board knew that it would take money to make it look professional.

A few members of the Board resigned. They did not want to commit to greater fundraising. They replaced themselves with higher ups in the business community. The Board meetings intensified in content and regularity. The growing pattern would be the usual; budget presented, pared down and presented again. Linda and I were asked to speak at fundraisers. It was part and parcel of the title we had. As co-directors, we carried overall responsibility for the success of the organization. Some members were with us from the beginning, some came aboard as the company turned professional. We needed them all and encouraged them all. Hopefully, one day it would get easier for us all!

The company toured the area with the opening night's program, switching casting to develop the group as a whole. I was preparing the program for the following season when the board informed us that it might be in the long term interest of the company to have alternating seasons. It would give them more time to develop a solid financial base. It was not an unreasonable concept but it was a difficult one to develop artistically. Inconsistent exposure does not build audiences.

We let the professionals go on extended leave, knowing we might not get them back again. In order to maintain visibility, we needed to prepare something for the spring with members of the academy. I came up with the idea of mounting a production of "Coppelia." The Board agreed. Though some roles would have to be hired in, most of the cast could be culled from the Academy. I knew this ballet from my days with ABT. The Board rented the set and costumes from Pittsburgh Ballet Theatre and booked the Wells Theatre in Norfolk for March performances. They were very happy with this plan. It was far less expensive than having to deal with the professional's salaries in addition to all other costs they incurred. They thought this a good interim plan. We, too, could live with it.

Linda and I decided that we would not dance in this production. We had danced "Three Preludes" in the professional season and Linda took the lead in "Rhapsody in Blue." We both wanted to inform the general public that we were finished "winding down." Not dancing in "Coppelia" would be our way of telling them. Our little girls from six years earlier were advanced, a few ready for professional companies, one already in Ballet Virginia. For the first time, we would be in the audience watching what we had created.

All performances of "Coppelia" were sold out in advance. The production looked wonderful on the Wells stage and one of our girls scored a much deserved success as Swanhilda, partnered by Jeff Satinoff of the Eliot Feld Ballet. The critics unanimously praised "Coppelia."

Before the next Board meeting the following week, the

finance manager of the company informed me that the production's budget had been LOANED from one of the local banks, one the president of the board was well connected to. The board had not raised any money for the agreed budget! The board was in debt for the entire production. After absorbing this news, I had time to talk about it with Linda before we met with the board. We could not condone this financially irresponsible behavior. We had been informed!

It was clear that this was as far as we could go in this area. The inability of the Board to raise money for the company told us there was no real future for the company. We either decided to remain an academy with student performances or resign our positions. We knew well what we were facing. It was what it was. We knew we had only one choice. We resigned our positions at the next board meeting.

Though the general reaction was sadness, there were signs of relief. Running a professional ballet company was very stressful for the Board. Our passion was their fantasy, not their passion. In the ensuing months before we departed to Boston, there was no indication that the board wanted to meet again. Our actions were justified by the inaction of the board. In retrospect, it was in the best interest of all: to date, twenty years later, there is no professional ballet company in that area. We sold the academy to a Balanchine-trained dancer who had worked on Broadway, put our house up for sale and made plans to move to Boston.

A surprise call from the Harvard University Summer dance program director came propitiously. She was in dire need of a ballet teacher. Could I help her out? Did I have room in my schedule? Could I? Did I? Though my plan was to teach at the Boston Ballet School, it could not begin until the fall. I was grateful for the interim engagement at Harvard University.

Several media interviews regarding the reasons behind our decision to leave the area were culminated with a final performance in Norfolk. It was a fundraising gala for the local Tidewater Ballet. They asked us to dance "Three Preludes," the ballet that brought us such enjoyment and acclaim. Our participation in the gala was highly publicized as our "final performance in the area." The event sold out! The audience was especially loving in their response to us, and the critics were nothing less than adulatory. The media-at-large made it very clear that our years spent in the area were enriching for all. As it turned out, this was not our final performance together. We would have one more performance to give.

Life After Plies

A request from the director of the Cape Cod Ballet to dance the roles of the Sugar Plum Fairy and the Nutcracker Prince in their production of "The Nutcracker" turned out to be our swan song. Watching the dancing of my favorite ballerina for the last time was the pure pleasure it had always been. If I didn't know that she was ready to hang up her pointe shoes, I would have thought she had years of good dancing remaining for her; so smooth was her movement, so fully dynamic was her interpretation, so musical was her motivation. Little Matthew brought the flowers onstage to his Mother. Sweeping him up in her arms, she gave her final bow before the public. I was right there behind them. She was his Mom and that role was new to her. Now she would have full time to get acquainted with it. For the first time since we were together, Linda had the opportunity not to work. Though it was very unusual, I was happy for her. I did not think it would be a lasting way of life for her but, for the time being, it was very nice indeed.

I was hired for a full- time position at the Boston Ballet School. Within weeks, I developed their first boy's class. I thought of those boys whom I taught in North Carolina during my time in the military. They were grown men now. I would like to think there was a professional dancer among them! I now had a chance to give it another go. I liked teaching. Dancing was the very best part of my career. The remaining options within a ballet career were limited to choreographing, directing or teaching. I was learning that teaching was a close second best for me.

It was very good for us to be back in a cosmopolitan, international city. Boston had all one needed and not too much of it. Its size had always impressed me. One could walk Boston. Harvard University was impressive certainly but it was also a very "cool" place to be around on a daily basis. Though I was ensconced in teaching far too many students from as many different countries during my six week engagement there, I was able to find time to absorb the atmosphere of the "halls of learning" and found the international quality of the area most impressive.

As a teacher in Boston, my accustomed workload was vastly reduced. I had time to play with Matthew and for us to sense family life. Matthew's effervescent personality was contagious. He was great fun to play with. He loved the physical contact of climbing on me and finding interesting ways to get down; his version of wrestling. We also did many balancing acts with me on my back and he in the starring role.

It was also a time for reading to him. His language skills were in place early. His questions were always appropriate. I created bedtime stories that were "to be continued…" night after night. The timing could not have been better. While he was so young and with our lives in transition, time together is what we needed. It was like a great present for all of us. Additionally, Linda was back where she grew up, with family and former friends inside and outside of the Boston Ballet. The next several months would be very interesting.

What would I have done if I had never been a dancer? This is a question most of us ask about this time in our careers. It is a question begging for an answer, a person wondering if there is another kind of work that would be compatible, if not comparable. After all, the instrument is older, the mind more developed and one's inquisitiveness alerted more than ever before. The thought process remains active while one goes about feeling his way.

Learning about the local dance scene brought some interesting results. I began to think in terms of dance presentation. I liked two smaller, local companies very much. I envisioned them touring the college circuit and smaller venues. To that end, I met with both groups. My teacher reputation preceded me. Some of their performers had taken my class at various times during our first year in Boston. In a smaller large city it doesn't take long to become known in the arts community.

Though these company managers were always interested in more bookings, they were not so sure I would be able to do more for them than they were already doing for themselves. It didn't take long for me to agree with that. The red tape involved in bookings, particularly where government monies were involved in the university circuit, would take up more time than I felt was wise to invest. It would take more time than I could offer before I would begin to see a return.

On a Sunday morning in August of 1988, I opened the want ad section of The Boston Globe. I was really very interested in putting myself out there, there in the work force of the general populace. I had never been there. I was curious. I also had another twenty years to offer. I was aware that a dancer can exercise such curiosity only if he is satiated with his dance experience. It was true that there was nothing in dance that I wanted to experience and did not. I wore all the hats. As a director/choreographer I produced fourteen ballets, three of which were full length productions. I was fully satisfied. The only thing left for me was to continue becoming the very best teacher I could be or change careers.

I perused the ads; ninety-five percent were ruled out because they required a four year college education and computer literacy. Then I saw one that could possibly work: WE WILL TRAIN, TOP POSITION WITH MAXIMUM EARNING POTENTIAL. NO PRIOR EXPERIENCE NEEDED, CALL NOW FOR AN APPOINTMENT! The key word there was TRAIN. It struck a chord with me as it would with any dancer.

Over the phone, the secretary gave me the time and place but not the nature of the work. I would learn that at the required meeting, she insisted. If I envisioned myself in another line of work altogether, this might be the opportunity, the only opportunity available to me. I decided to go to the "audition." I also decided to wait until I knew what it was about before speaking with Linda about it.

In suit attire I traveled to Wellesley Hills, MA, about ten miles west of Boston and met, along with many other people, the sales force of the Executive Fund from Van Nuys, California. After listening to an introduction regarding the insurance plans offered and the manner in which they trained individuals to sell them, we were broken up into groups. At the break, I thought I heard a voice calling. It was probably my Dad from Heaven saying to stay at the meeting a little longer. The fact that the atmosphere rang a bell was not to exaggerate.

I was interviewed by the manager. He complimented my appearance, telling me that I was selected to work in the Special Services section of the Fund's business. I would be given the names of thirty clients per week and propose enhancing their existing coverage with new insurance products. If I successfully added coverage to half of the leads, I would average a weekly paycheck of one thousand dollars! Could I begin the training for the state license on the following Monday? I agreed.

Linda, true to her cool manner when receiving sudden information, was not as surprised as I expected. I explained that I wanted to try this out. I was still on the ballet staff at the Boston Ballet but my days were free. She was as curious as I was to see if I would like doing this.

The hardest parts of the experience were the classes for license testing at University of Massachusetts. It had been a very long time since I was in an academic classroom. Weeks later, with license in hand, I felt like a new achiever. Could this be life after *plies*? Could this offer a better financial picture, going forward, than running all over Boston to teach enough classes to earn a living? With the housing costs in Massachusetts far exceeding other parts of the country, it was clear that we would need time before purchasing a home. For the time being, we would stay put in a rented apartment and watch how the "new" work developed for me.

The oomph I was getting from this possibility began to manifest itself. After the first sales, accompanied by a mentor, I was on my own. The audience was now across the table! I was making the money I was told I would make and I was closing nearly all the leads per week, every week. At the end of the first quarter, I was given the "Presidents Award" for being the "Ted Williams" of the sales force. I didn't yet know about Ted Williams. My numbers were impressive. I was their number one salesman!

I did like the work, particularly the independence associated with it. I would not have liked a job sitting at a desk. I was scheduling my week as I wanted it to be. I could see getting further involved. I would have to make a decision about my position at Boston Ballet. I couldn't see myself not somewhat involved in ballet but I could see myself taking a long hiatus.

A Second Career

A second career provides a second chance. Second chances are different; one is going in with a background, a life experience to offer. Though one was no longer able to expend kinetic energy in the same way a dancer does, that energy was forever a part of his psychological makeup. Re-channeling that energy would be the subconscious priority.

    Naturally, I felt the contrasting differences from dancing "Swan Lake" with London Festival Ballet to the insurance offices of The Executive Fund. Being in that blue stage light, partnering Linda's Odette was to feel the warmth of the stage, the security behind the stage makeup and costume, and the startling first sight of her birdlike creature entering the stage. Moving together to Tchaikovsky's music, we were in a stratosphere that only those who go there ever know.

That was then. It would never be again. What I was bringing to another career was all that and something else. I was interested in the "something else." This was now.

I had approached the work's scripting as though I was an actor. I was saying other people's words, finding my own way with them. I was aware that though I had been successful at this new work thus far, I was working with the clients of an insurance company. They were not my clients. I was not building a future for myself. The sales business had been in my family since my Mother met my Father. I decided to call my brother, Murph. That was a pivotal decision. Once he was satisfied that I actually wanted to continue along this path, he suggested that I become associated with a company where I could develop my own clientele. Given the Boston area, he suggested that I apply to the Sun Life of Canada Assurance Company, also in Wellesley, MA

The home office of this stellar, one hundred year old organization was located in Toronto. The Wellesley offices were the center for the United States operations. I presented myself as a former dancer but I also had my three months of Executive

Fund awards and numbers with me for the interview.

The initial ten minutes of the interview at Sun Life was spent with a sales manger. He then took me to the branch manager who was quick to point out that, "Though we don't know much about ballet dancers, we do know that they are disciplined and concentrated workers. We can always use those qualities here." He was happy to have my three month record to take to his higher ups. It would help him to secure the financing that I would need to begin building my own clientele with Sun Life products. There would be no "leads." One needed to build from "center of influence." With this in mind, I was offered a very reasonable package over a three year period, one with a sliding scale that would gradually decrease the monies they gave me as my own commissions kicked in. I was to build my own insurance business!

Center of Influence? I didn't have one. Being new in the area, I only knew dancers. They didn't have money to buy insurance. I was not likely to approach my in-laws and their relatives. Nepotism can so easily run afoul of original intentions. My clientele would have to be built slowly from new acquaintances and "cold calling," that oldest means of prospecting known to the art of the sale.

I remember well that when the poor results of my Aptitude Tests came back, the manager decided that he wanted me to be in the business regardless. He told me that I would be an insurance agent with a different sensibility, one who would add a new dimension to the office. Walking out of his office with contract in hand, I smiled, thinking it must have been the look in the suit again!

I decided I would make a full time effort in changing careers. I would not be teaching ballet; save the occasional private lesson for those I was committed to, or as a guest teacher now and then. I set out to build a "center of influence."

My new clientele became the other fathers at the local playground, new neighbors, an occasional former dancer and people I would meet who asked what it was I did for a living. The training at Sun Life was impressive, down to how one schedules his time, seven days a week. It was important to learn when to prospect, when to see clients, when to have family time, when to be alone. Without a structure, this was a chance to waste a great deal of time. Indeed, ninety-three percent of new hires are out of the business within a year. Furthermore, most that were successful, it turned out, were from other careers. In our office alone we had a superintendent of schools, several school teachers, two scientists, former office workers and a former ballet dancer!

Three mornings a week we learned and reviewed product; term life vs. whole life insurance, disability coverage, buy/sell agreements, annuities, estate planning, irrevocable trusts, second-to-die policies, universal life products, *etc.* One could get the equivalent of a degree in insurance right there in the office classroom. I was having my hand held. It was a period that would hold me in good stead for years to come.

I looked and moved differently than the average agent. Of course, the other agents as well as the secretaries wanted to talk about my former career and travels as often as I could offer the time. I felt the need to balance that with enough new business to earn my place there. The combination would prove to be winning.

Wonderful three year old Matthew was beginning nursery school. Linda was looking to begin a small teaching schedule around family time. We were finding our way in the Boston area, with work and parenting lifestyle. We looked to adopt a second child. Life was good, full of the feeling of a "second chance" about it. We spent time at the area beaches along Cape Cod as well as the North Shore. The quality of life in Massachusetts was very impressive. We set out to buy a home.

At the office, I slowly began to produce what I had been able to produce at the Executive Fund, without the leads. I enjoyed being my own boss. The manager gave praise to sales quotas met at each of the monthly office meetings. He focused on ways to improve one's market share, usually doing this more specifically in one on one conversation after the meetings.

"Bob, I wish I had you with me twenty years earlier", the manager stated as he acknowledged that he identified with me and the level of salesmanship I displayed. Of course there was greed as well as compliment in that statement; he took a piece of every agent's production. I replied, "Well, we still have twenty years ahead of us"!

The work presented a myriad of opportunities to meet all types of individuals. Through the years I have found that most people are reasonable, kind and welcoming if they need what the agent offered them. The concept hasn't really changed since man first sold something to another man. There is a dignity and certain fascination to the process. It is what it has always been: communication

"How can we use your background to further production and help the dance world at the same time?" asked the sales manager. I offered the idea of disability coverage to supplement workman's compensation payments. Heretofore, professional dancers and athletes were considered too high a risk for carriers to consider such a proposal.

Having read of some world celebrity's coverage with certain carriers, I suggested we find a carrier to take on the dance profession. Largely because of the sales manager's perseverance, we found American International Group (AIG) in New York to meet with us. AIG was the carrier for such superstars as Luciano Pavarotti and Madonna. I proposed a contract with benefits similar to those of Pavarotti's and Madonna's for the *corps de ballet*, relative of course to income vs. expense. They took my criteria, along with the numbers of professional companies and dancers, back to their drawing boards. They did not say no.

With the help of the American Guild of Musical Artists (AGMA), the dancer's union whose president happened to be my former dance agent, we put the group plan in place. It took all of six months time. I was established as the General Agent for the plan. The year was 1991. I began to travel between Boston and New York weekly, meeting with dancers backstage at Lincoln Center in between matinee and evening performances. These meetings were for the soloists and principals whose incomes warranted individual policies. Of course it was fun to be with former colleagues again and wonderful to be able to bring to them the same security that the rest of the nation's workforce had long enjoyed. The companies on the West Coast and in the Midwest were managed via telephone, fax and correspondence.

The news of this historic event made the cover of DANCE MAGAZINE's September issue. I felt that I was "giving back" to a profession that was good to me and that I loved first. An even better feeling came a few years later when the dancer's union decided to have the ballet companies provide the supplement in the dancer's contracts. I had been able to be a catalyst to a new permanence for all future dancers. There would be no more need for the insurance carrier.

Three years had passed since I made the career change. I was in for the long run. The relentless aspect of the business had been accepted. It was never about what you did yesterday but about what you were going to do today. It was up to the individual to find the work. I thanked my dance training, ballet career and military experience for developing my work ethic. If life was work, it was alright by me. I was not one to look for a short cut or to skip a beat in the process. I knew that skipping B to get to C only meant that one day you'd have to go back and get that B. I was not one to waste time like that.

The Gift of Music

Music, being the reason why I danced, was the gift I wanted to give to Matthew. For this purpose, the only item brought to Massachusetts from The Dance Academy in Virginia was the better of our two pianos.

    I set out to learn what age a child should be before beginning piano lessons. I learned this information and more by signing up for beginner lessons myself. I learned how to play the piano! I had always wanted to learn how to play; would always be the one at the side of the pianist in ballet rehearsals whenever I wasn't actually dancing.

The teacher was encouraging to her class of insurance agents, secretaries, medical professionals, professors, *etc*. We were guaranteed to play with two hands and sight read at the end of the eight week course. It not only worked but was stimulating enough that most of us wanted to go onto Adult Piano II.

I asked her about the proper age for a child to begin lessons. She said the younger the child the better, before one lost interest to the many other distractions available to the young minds of the day. She drew a correlation between the study of music and the study of language. She was referring specifically to the Suzuki Piano teaching method. She went on to informed me that one of the best teachers in the area happened to be in the city where we lived. I arranged for a time to meet with him and to observe his students. I was impressed with such young children getting the benefit of musical training and that they played well. He gave me the Suzuki theory book, "Nurtured by Love" and told me to call him after I had read the book.

This impressive book dealt with the belief that all children who are not deaf can play a musical instrument, that all children are talented. The method worked by playing the Suzuki musical tapes in the home, along with normal activities. The child would practice what he HEARD, with the parent, for five to ten minutes a day. There would be one fifteen minute class a week where they did age appropriate activities such as jumping on a giant plastic keyboard, which served as a floor covering, to identify the notes being played by the teacher. It was clearly a sound manner in which to involve a young mind along with sports related activities, *etc*. I spoke with Linda about this technique and we agreed that the three of us should make a visit to the teacher.

Like the majority of young children, Matthew learned quickly. I had been speaking to him in Spanish since he was very young; he was not only responsive but developed a very good accent as well. The miracle of the sponge- like mind of the young was captivating indeed. In June, 1990, two months before Matthew turned five, we began piano lessons.

That same year we purchased the home we now live in, nine miles from Boston. After our move, Matthew had his first recital. He played two pieces, bowed and came back to sit with us in the audience. After the recital, one heard and made remarks about the students. The one comment from the teacher about Matthew's playing was that he had a natural left hand; his sense of the "piano" quality in playing was a gift. Everyone commented on the expressiveness of his playing. These two qualities were what we would hear repeatedly throughout the next ten years of his training.

The following year, we identified a teacher who taught in the traditional "sight reading" method. It was already clear to us that if one remained with the Suzuki method beyond the initial years, one would not develop sight reading ability. After

Matthew's second annual recital, I had the idea to arrange monthly "piano parties." It seemed a better preparation for the annual recital if the students had the opportunity to play before a smaller audience more regularly during the year and where they could associate the inherent work with fun. With the teacher's permission, we began to have these parties in the student's homes. Everyone became involved and, by and large, the parties were quite successful.

By the age of ten, Matthew had developed a small repertoire. He had been working with the music of the major composers for some time. Though he did not like to practice and wasn't particularly keen on lessons, he played very well. I wondered if we should continue with lessons at this point. I grew more curious to see what other teacher's opinions of his work would be. We took him to the New England Conservatory of Music in Boston for the assessment.

After playing three pieces, we heard what we were used to hearing about his playing; the natural, expressive playing, *etc.* He was given a partial scholarship to join the preparatory department there. The main reason we considered having him study at the Conservatory was that they gave recitals on a monthly basis and the adjudication was done by teachers who did not know the students. It was a very interesting concept and produced equally interesting results.

Matthew's musical study had given us the experience of

live music being played daily in the home. His natural ability did not belie the fact that he was not interested in working at the piano. If I had illusions about hearing him play an evening of Chopin Nocturnes and Sonatas at Carnegie Hall one day they were, in time, dispelled. For Matthew, having a natural talent was one thing; wanting to have a career at playing the piano was another. He did not want to do that. During his years at the piano we were also involved in school sports, my taking the position of Coach on his basketball team one year. He competed on a local swim team throughout his middle school years. By the time high school came around, he was very interested in wrestling and football. We were "nurturing." He was "naturing."

He continued piano studies well into his high school years, giving some of his most heartfelt renderings in the monthly recitals that took place at the conservatory. Time gave way to other interests. Continuing at the Conservatory would require him to spend a lot more time at the piano. It was then that the formal lessons stopped. He was a trained pianist, satisfied with his musical accomplishments. It is his lifetime gift.

Professionally, I had been experiencing the effects of the recession that had gripped Massachusetts over the previous years. With the unemployment rate staggeringly high, housing costs far above the nation's average and rental space down to five dollars a square foot, people and businesses began to leave the state in droves. They were going where they could find work and affordable housing. For many of them, that meant a move to the southern part of the country.

Many of those people were insurance clients who could no longer pay their premiums; they forfeited their policies and the agent's commissions along with them. The company policy of paying a full year's commission on a monthly, quarterly or semi annual premium payment put many of us in jeopardy. Those commissions were retracted by pro rating. One owed the balance. All events compounding, we found ourselves in serious financial difficulties for the first time. Family and friends came through to help us over the next year. With their help, I was able to rebuild my clientele over the next few years.

One of my favorite "people" experiences came about at this time. After the career change, it had become a natural fact that people were interested in knowing that my first career was on the ballet stage. This always occurred during the normal course of conversation exchange. No one took quite the interest like Cynthia did. She had the background to more fully appreciate ballet as well as my career change. She was a balletomane whose favorite dancers were Fonteyn and Nureyev. A former employee at the United Nations, she was also listed in Who's Who of American Women for her work on behalf of the Native Americans and the environment; an interesting person in her own right.

During our initial meeting at a picnic table outside the office park where we both worked (she as a "temp" at the time), she learned that, during my ballet career, I worked alongside both of her favorite dancers. She was very happy to meet a former professional dancer there in the office complex. She was also quite lonely. I later learned that she had recently lost her significant other. Nearing seventy years of age, she seemed like she could use some new friends. At the next lunch meeting, she told me that she researched what I had told her about myself. I liked that. She was informed by members of the Boston dance community that I was the real McCoy!

I took the initiative to have her meet Linda and Matthew, to let her come into our lives and to give her a sense of family, something she did not have. My kindness to her was gratefully received and she has been a kind and generous friend to our family throughout the years. The highlight of our friendship manifested itself in my encouraging Cynthia to take up the offer from a certain Charles in Pennsylvania who had unexpectedly proposed to her. She had not been married for forty years, having divorced a Danish count after a brief early marriage. Charles was a widower for the second time. He had the means to offer Cynthia security. They were married the following year. She was sixty-nine and he was seventy. We were very proud of them both!

That initial meeting at the picnic table, with ballet being the mutual interest, holds a special memory for me. To this day I summarize our friendship as symbolizing the mixing of the former and current careers with a lasting friendship built on the understanding of both. She is the only friend of whom I can say that.

A Thickening Waistline

How could this be? I was losing my waistline! I wasn't sitting at a computer all day long. I was in and out of the office most of the time. At home I was kept busy caring for our three-story home and its property. It had to be the aging process, later to be referred to as "processing!" I needed to get involved in regular exercise. A health club seemed the logical place to begin.

The nearest and best equipped club was easily accessible. It was on the way home from the office. I decided to take a day pass at The Lexington Health Club. It was a very cold

December day in 1995. Walking around the facility, I stopped to observe a high impact aerobics class that was just beginning. I watched as they began jumping about without warming up. Without considering that I might not be alone, I said aloud "What they need first is a good ballet *barre*." The lady with the long red braid standing next to me replied, "Well, who do you know that could provide that for them?"

This was Suzanne, the club's fitness director. After explaining myself, she asked me if I could send her my resume. Suzanne was cleary interested. She had a background in dance and thought the idea of a ballet class for the club would be sensational. Before I left the club she showed me one of their studios. In it were ballet *barres* and mirrors! She called it the "stretch" studio.

About ten days later, Suzanne called my office inquiring what day I wanted to start the club's first Adult Ballet Class. She went on to tell me that she had shown the resume to two club members who happened to be former dancers. They insisted that she "give him whatever he wants, do whatever it takes to get him. He is a 'Prince' of the ballet!" It had been a long time since I had garnered a review and never one quite like that!

The thought came to me of how appropriate it seemed; I could reacquaint my body with basic positions again, achieve some of that long lost muscular isolation AND bring a new discipline to the health club. Given my then current schedule, the class would have to be on Wednesday mornings at 10:30. She had the spot open. We set January 8, 1996 for the first class.

Flyers went up and the questions began. Who is he? Will this be "real" ballet? Adult ballet classes had not been offered in the health club industry before though such classes had gained popularity at local dancing schools. In major cities there were classes for adults on a regular basis.

Eight club members came to the first class. The former dancers were there, and four of the others looked like they could have been. All were familiar with working their bodies. Immediately I sense that, though they may be apprehensive about what I would ask them to do, they were ready to try. I would soon learn that, with few exceptions, this would be the normal approach with health club members. They looked a whole lot better than many of adult class attendees that I had taught.

The class was well received. The members were very grateful for the class to be scheduled right there in their club. The word spread that the class was indeed "real" and that the teacher took the members seriously. By the fourth class, the attendance had doubled. The management was impressed with Suzanne and Suzanne was impressed with me. I was beginning to feel muscular isolation again. It had been eight years since I was an active dancer.

The members could not get enough of the class. I was

restructuring my teaching technique for these adults. I knew we needed to organize a second class. One could not do any discipline only one time a week. It was a matter of when. My only possibility was Fridays at 11:30am. Suzanne was doubtful. "This is an affluent community and many of the members take three day weekends. It won't work on Fridays" she moaned. I persevered. Fridays became more popular than Wednesdays; the members began their three day weekend AFTER ballet class!

    The myriad of stories I heard from the members regarding their start with dance lessons, their always having wanted to start classes or the number of years it has been since they took a class would extend the length of this book beyond reason. It suffices to say that they were wholly taken up with the music of the class, the French terminology of the technique and the fact that I instructed in a manner that made them feel validated. In time, the all important beneficial aspects of creating such a class in one's later years would be manifested in many ways.

    For the time being their remarks centered on the benefit of not thinking about anything else for one solid hour, that "it was great therapy and a whole lot cheaper than going to a shrink." Their friends began remarking on their improved carriage. Inevitably a third class had to be arranged.

    Several times in a row, I had noticed potential club members peering through the classroom windows from the hallway. They were doing the same thing I did when I first entered the club – perusing. They would return to the front desk with the exclamation that "Everyone in that class knows what they are doing; they all have the same arm up at the same time! I will never catch up." Their words got back to me. I decided the club needed a "new beginner" class for those who did not know the First Position of ballet technique. Otherwise, we would be turning away too many potential members. My schedule was down to bare bones. It would have to be Mondays at 12:30pm.

    This class became the most popularly attended of the three. Now we had a new beginner, a beginner/intermediate and an intermediate on Monday, Wednesday and Friday respectively. The class size was nearing twenty-five. I decided to write a "how to" guide geared toward studio owners who were not sure what to give the moms and pops in an adult ballet class. It would contain a curriculum, proper room and class size recommendations, as well as recommendations for the class length and frequency during the week. I would include a sample class.

    The reputation of the class was very high among the members and club staff. People were walking taller whenever they saw me. I was gearing in on the alignment of the body during the class, learning that at any age one can benefit from standing and walking in alignment. With proper body alignment, the energy level would improve, blood circulation would be better and oxygen had a much easier time getting in to do its wonders. I could see the results before they remarked upon them. The first two years established the future growth of the class and my work in it. My waistline also improved! However, a forced sabbatical was in store!

Beach Drive, one incredibly pretty mile-long road that led from the town of Manchester-by-the-Sea to the Atlantic Ocean, was very familiar to us during the summer months. It led to Singing Beach. Our other favorite spot was Kennebunkport, Maine, where we also spent time each summer.

As was our habit, I would drop the others at Singing Beach before taking the car back to town for parking. I would then ride the bike we always brought with us up Beach Drive to the beach. Before we were ready to "get going," I would take the bike back to the car, return and retrieve the others. This ritual was done tens and tens of times and was always something I particularly looked forward to.

During the summer of 1998, on one of those bike runs, I didn't make it back to the car. Suddenly I was sitting on Beach Drive holding my bloody face in my hands. I had gone head first over the handle bars and, from reports of the people walking up the road to the beach, the bike then flipped over me. The people immediately helped me. It was mid afternoon. Some of those beach-going people were asking me questions. I was able to give them the car keys to bring to Linda who was waiting for me at the beach rotary. Matthew and a friend of his were with her.

The next thing I remember hearing was "Dad, it's Matt. I'll get the bike, Dad." His unsettling voice revealed his shocking reaction. The emergency crew was quickly on the scene, taking me to the nearest hospital. The injuries to my face were serious. While on the ride to the hospital, the crew called the plastic surgeon that was on call that day.

"I am so sorry this happened to you but I have to tell you that you have great capillaries!" said the very attractive female doctor before me. She thought it best that the boys did not come in to see me, telling Linda that she was free to take them home. I was going to be in surgery for "awhile." Linda had already seen me. When the doctor learned that I was a dance teacher, she asked me to promise her Tango lessons once I recuperated. I didn't let on that the Tango was the one dance that the Arthur Murray teachers didn't teach me!

Four and a half hours later, I was in the recovery room remembering only the male nurse's and the anesthesiologist's remarks, as I was dozing off, that I could well have been the "Christopher Reeve" of the day. I was lucky to have fallen in such a relaxed manner. Normally, such a fall breaks the neck.

My face was lacerated by the fall, the nose was pulverized and four of my front teeth were left on Beach Drive. I began a nine week healing period where I not only did not teach a ballet class, I also did not see a client. Furthermore the treatments, which included oral surgery, were exceptionally well performed.

However, none compared to the level of my new nurse, Linda DiBona. What a quick study she was! With two lessons in the hospital about how one cleans face wounds, and rebandage them, she was on her way; Florence Nightingale herself! It was requested that she do this four times a day. Though I had pain medication, I don't recall depending on it nor do I recall pain. I became very interested in the healing process to the point of finding it a spiritual experience. I thought about looking into the mirror but I didn't.

A large part of my healing had to do with the love and expressions of well wishers. I was very taken aback by the degree to which friends were affected by my accident. The family reaction was a given but the friends and associates made a deep impression. Their concern and feeling for me healed me.

When the first visit to the oral surgeon drew a scream from the receptionist, I really should have known enough to become immediately depressed. Instead Linda and I got a laugh out of it. One could not have staged that moment if they tried. We really felt sorry for the girl. Soon I would get a chance to see what she saw. I decided to look into a mirror. I could see that, if not exactly Frankenstein, it was bad. It just wasn't me, not yet.

After some weeks, the plastic surgeon was anxious to have another go at it, feeling that she could make her good work even better. I thought about that and realized that a "perfect" reconstruction would be much more important had it been twenty years earlier and I was in the middle of my ballet career. I was pleased with what she was able to do without having even a photo to work from. The nose looked perfectly like mine though there would be some facial scarring and I would have the upper lip revised at a later date.

Once back at the office, I learned that business was not going as well as Sun Life wanted it to go. This was basically the results of an agency system that was too expensive to maintain. Compared to a brokerage company receiving business from a huge pool of brokers, an agency needed large volumes of business from fewer captive agents to cover greater overhead costs. Our branch was notified that the home office would be changing the way they did business. They offered the agents to become brokers, remain where they were, pay the costs of running their own business to Sun Life and, in return, Sun Life would double commissions.

The problem with that scenario was that the company did not know the brokerage system. Sixty-five percent of us opted to open our own brokerage office, taking on a brokers' license and providing our own benefits. With the technology of the day easily making one's home office a virtual business space, it seemed the better the way to go. The commissions would double nonetheless but, this way, one was in charge of the costs of doing his business the way he wanted to do it, not the company's way. My business, INSURANCE PLANNING, was established in1997.

Of all the possibilities that my imagination could envision, having my own insurance business one day was not one of them. Ability like any talent is, of itself, not much. Combined with training and disciplined work ethic, ability can become interesting. Add passion to the mix and the horizon can look very far and wide indeed.

How does a dancer apply passion to the corporate world? For me, the answer was the love of people. It seems reasonable that one would not place himself before the public in any manner if he did not want to improve their lots. Did a ballet performance of mine leave the viewer better off than they were before the performance? Did I leave a client better off than I found him? Was the passion of the personality involved in both realities? You bet!

My business was comprised of a clientele with a wide financial range. There was the client who paid a forty-six thousand dollar annual premium to have her estate protected by an insurance trust. That case provided me with a twenty-five thousand dollar commission. There was the client who could not manage to keep up payments on his annual premium of five hundred and fifty dollars, whose policy I reduced and whose annual payment I changed to monthly mode so that he would have "some" coverage. The majority of my clients have fallen somewhere in the middle. They have all been the culmination of working with the public at large and only deferring business if the proposed client was disagreeable. In this business the agent can be faulted for using undue pressure or misrepresentation, both of which can result in the loss of his license to do business. Sometimes, a potential client can be deemed unworthy of due process. Very seldom have I chosen not to work in such circumstances.

    I remember taking the call from the father of a young widow, whose coverage for her and her husband I had put in force only two years earlier. He told me that she did not want to go to her husband's wake: she wanted to talk with me first. Would I please call her? She needed diversion from grief. I managed to help her to the wake. Of course, I had resource for that one. I remembered my Mother resisting my Father's wake!

    Each case I undertook was different from the other. I understood that it wasn't very different from the diversity of people in a theatre audience. What were the resources that I could bring to the table? I found that there were many and that THEY are the rewards of having lived the life that I had lived so far. Combining one's sensibility for a given situation with his life experience created empathy, generosity and trust; a developed personality was in the offering.

A Knock on the Door

In March of 2000, I was diagnosed with a cancerous tumor in my breast. I hadn't even considered that men had breasts. Certainly most people had not heard of breast cancer in men. I was soon to be enlightened. Men do have breasts. What they don't have is active mammary glands.

I was showering when I noticed a hard lump next to my left nipple. Afterward, I asked Linda to feel it. She agreed that it be checked out immediately. My doctor insisted that the breast surgeon see me at once. Though the surgeon was fairly confidant that this mass was benign, he ordered a biopsy for the end of the week. The mass taken from my breast was 3.5 centimeters in size. Inside the mass was a 1.7 centimeter tumor. I awaited the pathology report.

I remembered an experience I had during puberty; I had felt a lump in that same area when I was eleven years old. The doctor at the time explained to me that it was just a part of my "body change." Could this be coincidental? When I told my surgeon of this recollection he responded, "If you want me to tell you, Bob, how this mass occurred, I will give you an answer. However, I want you to know that none of us really knows that answer, only He knows (pointing upward). I will tell you that I think it is due to a hormonal change." He went onto explain that as men "process" they lose testosterone and accumulate estrogen; the opposite of what happens to women during menopause. He theorized that the growth in my breast was generated when the estrogen kicked in.

For Linda this was the second of what would be three events within eight months that would threaten the men in her life. Two weeks before my diagnosis, her brother, Donald, died of Scleroderma. Being her only brother whose only nephew was Matthew, Donald held a special place in our family. Six months after my episode, Linda's father died of lung complications at the age of eighty-nine. This ended a sixty-three year marriage and the life of the patriarchal head of the family.

The pathology report revealed that my tumor was cancerous; stage-two adenocarcinoma.

As others have described before me, learning that one had a cancerous tumor is an out of body experience. This was best exemplified when I was getting dressed just after the surgeon finished changing my bandage while telling me the results of the pathology report. He was surprisingly despondent. I expected his long experience to come to the fore but it didn't. He said that my being a dancer made him very sad because he had more to tell me. He recommended surgery that would likely result in partially paralyzing my left arm.

I told him that I wanted to call my wife to tell her the results. "No, you will go home and talk with your wife!" he replied.

He had explained the importance of having a radical mastectomy; the only sure way to know if the cancer had spread. He was clear in telling me that the procedure would render my left arm twenty-five percent paralyzed. He gave me the names of the oncologist, chemotherapist and radiation specialists he wanted me to speak with as well. As I finished tying my tie, we left the office, walking in separate directions. I looked back at him. He was walking with his head bowed very low.

Approaching the elevator, I noticed that each person I passed was staring at me. How did they know? The staring continued in the elevator and on the way to the car. It happened at each traffic light. Does one have the message, "I HAD A CANCEROUS TUMOR," on his forehead as soon as one learns about it? Only when I was near home, did I take a moment to look well into the review mirror. Then I saw it. My tie was perfectly tied on the OUTSIDE of my collar; my overt sign of the out of body experience. The doctor had watched me tie the tie!

I adjusted the tie before I got into the house. The news was taken bravely but that was only for my benefit. She was perhaps less terrified because I was, by that time, somewhat under control. I had had my moment. She needed to have hers and we needed to have ours together. I thought of the friend who told me of asking her spouse if he could live without her. Suddenly this seemed to be a very important question. I didn't know what life would be like without Linda. She might have to think about living without me in her life. I so wanted us to be able to say that, though it would be very different, it would be okay. It was not that easy and it was not discussed again.

Instinctively, I knew that I would not opt for a mastectomy. I would not opt to live life without all the faculties I was accustomed to. We decided to meet with the other specialists to see what they had to recommend.

Chemo was a poison that would surely interfere with whatever immune system was naturally at work in my body, radiation was likely to burn a part of the heart because the tumor had been on the left side. Neither of these would be as effective as the paralyzing surgery.

My thoughts ventured far and wide. What an interesting experience life had been for me! The length of one's life seemed far less important than how one lived that life. The quality of my life far outweighed any extra number of years without that quality. The fact that I may not have a cancerous disease but did have a cancerous tumor removed became my starting rational. In time, I would either know the repeat manifestations of Cancer or I would be one of the fortunate people who did not develop the disease. I was willing to take that chance. I hoped others, especially those who loved and knew me well, would understand my rationale. For the time being, I felt every bit as well as I had before the diagnosis. I took advantage of a second opinion. That gave me the strength to face the doctors with my decision not to opt for any radical treatment.

After each expressed their dismay with my decision, the oncologist insisted that I take the oral medication, Tamoxifen. Within a week, I began to develop the medicine's side effects of swollen legs and feeling as though I was "walking cotton." I had been warned of these possibilities. I stopped taking the medicine.

For five years, four times a year, I have had blood drawn, been screened for other possible carcinomas and have been regularly examined by my oncologist. Once a year for five years I have had a mammogram. At the end of five years, I was considered to be in recession. I am now in my seventh year. I often think of my surgeon who told me that he often doesn't have the answers he is expected to have. I viewed the cancer occurrence as a cosmic knock on my door. The same thought then occurred to me that I had after the bicycle accident: In the grand scheme of things, my work is not done. There is more for me to do.

I befriended cancer. I did not fight or want to battle it. I talked about it with whoever wanted to know, especially men. Though I know, on a daily basis, that a re-occurrence is a possibility, I still trust my body. I am always a dancer.

Results

My adult ballet classes have grown in size. The number of attending club members generally maximizes the space we have to work in. The results of continuous work on the body alignment, using the classical ballet technique, have proven beneficial for all. Those who make three classes per week benefit the most. Many have told me that they have stopped seeing their doctor(s), stopped taking pain killing medication(s) and have generally improved health. They attribute this directly to the work they do in the class. Certainly it is, in large part, just that. I have learned along with them that the importance of good posture, from which exercise movements should radiate, cannot be overstated at any age.

The group age range is from thirty to seventy-five. The professional makeup of the class includes Dolores, an artist, Dorit, an architect, Michael, a dentist/entrepreneur, Carol, a sculptress, Kathy, a professional learner, Donna, a language specialist, Shayna, a graphic designer, Fred, a retired engineer, Alice, a retired teacher, Elaine, a former nurse, Linda, a painter, Leslie, a former dancer/teacher, Babs, a real estate broker, Diana, a fitness instructor, Ann, a former dancer, Barbara, a teacher, Rong, a scientist, Ginny, a hairstylist, Jane, an engineer, Marsha, a world traveler, Christine, a videographer, Ellen Beth, an inventor, Judith, a former girls camp counselor, Merry, a psychologist, Ellen, a special needs teacher, Mindy, a yoga instructor, Helen, a homemaker, Carol, a singer, Karen, an economist, Janet, a software developer, Michelle, a lawyer/ballroom dancer as well as all the others who have similar backgrounds. And on the rare occasion, my beautiful wife graces this class with her presence, reminding me that I continue to be inspired by her.

All of these people and those who have taken the classes over the past ten years have shown their gratitude consistently and have been very generous with their expressions. It is a continuous pleasure to bring to their lives something of importance, to be a messenger of that which is greater than us. All teachers of an art-form have this opportunity.

My life is a reconfirmation of everything I have learned

from dancing. It continues to be reconfirming. I am now looking back at the life that not only provided the prerequisites of family, health, food on the table, comfort in the home but also included an unusual amount of adventure early on. It is a life that encompasses early tragedy as well as opportunities, surviving wartime, marrying a ballerina, and becoming a "prince." It is one that provided more adventure while dancing throughout much of the world, directing a school and dance company, choreographing a dozen ballets and becoming an adoptive father. The "second" professional career that I have forged with a dancer's confidence provides further pleasures of serving the public, of parenting, of growing gardens as well as friendships. I continue to be afforded the opportunity to use what I have learned for the benefit of others. Mostly, it is a life privileged to have been inspired by the art of dance.

In all good theatre there is the great moment of surprise. For me, that moment continues in the fact that I have lived much of my life while being loved by the same woman. Among other things, she has represented the fact that one does nothing in life alone.

Through daily living, I am regularly reminded that the gift of dance has been useful throughout my entire life. People have loved me for it. Its lessons are forever supporting my endeavors. I am always looking to give back; one's rewards really should be recycled!

If I were to choose yet a third career, it would be done with the attitude of confidence honed by the continuous sense of satisfaction I have derived from being a dancer. I see a seemingly endless horizon ahead, yet I am already twice as old as I ever thought I would be.

For that and for the many people who have helped me along the way, there seems no better gesture of appreciation than to be always a dancer.

Epilogue

"Pass through slowly, scratching your ankles. Be sure to keep the light between the two of you; this is an embraceable dance. We like each other."

    I found the Argentine Tango lessons I had long been looking for. Now it was scheduled on the right night of the week for both of us, with a guest instructor from Buenos Aires. It was not Ballroom tango, it was not European tango, it was Argentine tango. It was about leading and following, rhythm and communion, about embracing movement in space to music. The feet were parallel. The dance was quiet in its integrity. It was challenging. I was back where I belonged. Learning is the act of life for me. I had been teaching about life, dancing, whatever I thought I knew well; the act of transferring information. I was hungry to learn again. The light between the two of us was bright. We would keep that light, ever changing in its intensity, always easily rediscovered. It was the light of true love; the light of dance.

"Ability like any talent is, of itself, not much. Combined with training and disciplined work-ethic, ability can become interesting. Add passion to the mix and the horizon can look very far and wide indeed"

                                                           The Author

Index

AAUW, 178
A Chorus Line, 23
AGMA, 200
AIG, 199
American Ballet Center, 28
American Ballet Theatre, 33, 43, 65, 70, 79
Americana Hotel, 26, 28, 162
Ailey, Alvin, 85
Aldige River, 88
Algaroff, Youly, 134
Alonso, Alicia, 160
A Midsummer Night's Dream, 180
Anatassoff, Cryil, 135
Anderson, Connie, 104, 169, 170
Apartheid, 150
Apollo Theatre, 31
Appel, Peter, 170
Arena di Verona, 88
Arpino, Gerald, 43

Ashford and Simpson, 83
Astarte, 69
Atlas Mountains, 139
Baez, Joan, 118
Bain, Wilfred C., 45
Baird Hall, 68
Balanchine, George, 23, 27, 38
Ballet Arts, 164
Ballet Beranger, 134, 138
Ballet d'Opéra du Nice, 134
Ballet du Wallonie, 160
Ballet International, 147
Ballets Russes, 23, 81, 99, 132
Ballet van Vlaanderen, 131, 134
Ballets USA, 41
Ballet Virginia, 178, 182
Baryshnikov, Mikhaïl, 117
Basel Ballet, 168
Bennett, Michael, 23, 25
Berra, Yogi, 118
Bizet, 182

Bolshoi Ballet, 24, 79
Bogaerts, Marc, 182
Boston Ballet, 39, 76, 169, 189, 193
Boston Ballet School, 186, 188
Brabants, Jeanne, 131, 134, 170
Brassel, Matthew Robert, 181
Bruhn, Erik, 80, 85
Buffalo General Hospital, 67
Burke, Ginger, 21
Bushmen, 154
Butler, John, 39, 76, 133
Cape Cod Ballet, 187
Cape of Good Hope, 153
Capetown Gazette, 153
Caramoor Festival, 39, 76
Carnegie Hall, 29, 164, 206
Carter, Jimmy, 153
Cecchetti, 179
Central Park, 44, 58
Champs Élysée, 119
Chapel Hill, 52

Chase, Lucia, 71, 79, 85, 96
Chopin, 206
City Center Joffrey Ballet, 69, 70
Clouser, James, 72
Club Mediterranean, 159
Como, Bill, 182
Connecticut Ballet, 180
Covent Garden, 87
Credit Suisse, 104
Cunningham, Merce, 35
Dade County Auditorium, 124
Dance Magazine, 54, 182, 200
Danielian, Leon, 71
Danner, Blythe, 83
Danse Perspective, 134
Delacorte Theatre, 44, 57
DeMille, Agnes, 80, 81
Diaghilev, 81
DiBona, Linda, 40, 75, 77, 121
Difiglia, Micky, 23
Dominican Republic, 178
Don Quixote, 141, 142
Douglas, Scott, 80

East China Sea, 57
Eglevsky, Andre, 99
Eliot Feld Ballet, The, 184
Ellington, Duke, 85
Encyclopedia Americana, 2
Encyclopedia Britannica, 11
Eva's Boutique, 91
Executive Fund, 191, 194, 195
Feld, Eliot, 80
Fernandez, Royes, 80
Fitzgerald, Ella,
   30, 114, 118, 161
Fonteyn, Margot, 37, 38, 145
Foxy, 38, 39
Fracci, Carla, 80, 88
Franchetti, Frano, 135
Ft. Belvoire, 56
Ft. Bragg, 50, 54, 55, 56, 106
Ft. Dix, 50
Ft. McCallum, 50
Garden State Ballet, 71
Gaudi, Antonio, 91
Gershwin, 182
Giselle, 71, 80, 84, 96

Good, H.L., 87
Gore, Walter, 95
Goslar, Lotte, 42
Graham, Martha, 42
Granada, 160
Gregory, Cynthia, 79
Grey, Dame Beryl, 135
Gucci, 26
Harkness Ballet, The, 42
Harkness House for
   Ballet Arts, 105
Harkness, Rebekah, 41, 121, 171
Harvard University, 186, 188
Harvard University
   Summer Dance, 185
Herod Atticus Theatre, 89
Hluhluwe Game Reserve, 157
Holland, Dozier and Holland, 83
Hunter College, 76
Hynd, Ronald, 145
Indiana University, 45, 46, 64
Insurance Planning, 219
International Herald
   Tribune, 117, 122

Iranian International
  Ballet Festival, 165
Iranian National Ballet, 166
Jacob's Pillow Dance Festival, 43
Joffrey, Robert, 27, 66
Johannesburg Press, 149
Johnson's, Howard, 22
Kamen, Michael, 113, 123
Kelly, Gene, 78
John F. Kennedy Center for
  the Performing Arts, 94
Kennedy, Robert, 45
Kirov Ballet, 117
Kiss Me Kate, 20, 68
Koesun, Ruthann, 80
Kriza, Johnny, 80
L.E.M.Co, 16th (GS), 55
  (DS), 56
La Bayadere, 37, 165
Labis, Attilio, 160
Lahr, Bert, 38
Lander, Herald, 82
Lander, Toni, 79
Lawrence of Arabia, 139

Le Grand Ballet du Geneve, 160
Le Monde, 134
Le Orangerie, 69, 70, 71, 72
Library for the
  Performing Arts, 34
Limon, Jose, 85
Lincoln Center, 34
Lland, Michael, 33
London Coliseum, 145
London Festival Ballet, 135, 194
Long, Larry, 147
Longchamps, 35
M-16 rifle, 49
M*A*S*H, 96
Macdonald, Brian, 113
MacLaine, Shirley, 20
Madonna, 199
Markova, Alicia, 36, 66
Martin, Max, 147
Masai Tribe, 157
Massine, Leonide, 80
Maxim's, 136
McLain, David, 33
Menegatti, Beppe, 88

Metropolitan Opera, 92
Metropolitan Opera Ballet, 28, 36
Mingus, Charlie, 118
Mink Mountain, 166
Moore, James, 103
Moore, Lillian, 33
Motown, 51, 83
Motte, Claire, 134
Murray, Arthur, 14, 216
Myers, Mike, 174
Nahat, Dennis, 80
National Ballet of Canada, 20
New Ballet School, 173
New England Conservatory, 205
New Haven Ballet, 33
Newman, Paul, 91, 92
Newsweek Magazine, 37
New York City Ballet,
   23, 45, 46, 174
New York State Theatre, 85
New York Theatre
   Workshop, 164
Nico Milan Theatre, 151
Nightingale, Florence, 217

North Carolina School
   of the Arts, 173
Nureyev, Rudolph 37, 38
Nutcracker, The,
   34, 109, 149, 169, 187
Nutured by Love, 203
Oakland Air Base, 60
Oakland Ballet, 180
O'Keefe Center, 24
Okinawa, 57, 60, 89, 109
Olympics, 52
O'Toole, Peter, 139
PACOFS, 151, 155
Paltrow, Bruce, 83
PaperMill Playhouse, 110
Paris Opera, 134
Park Savoy Hotel, 28
Pavarotti, Luciano, 199
Pavlavi Family, 166
Pennsylvania Ballet, 99
Pereyaslavec, Valentina, 71
Pittsburgh Ballet Theatre, 184
Plisetskaya, Maya, 24
Pontois, Noella, 135

Porter, Cole, 20
Poughkeepsie Ballet
  Theatre, 165
Pourfarrokh, Ali, 166
Prudential Life, 16
Queen Elizabeth II, 87
Quinn, Anthony, 90
Reed, Gilbert and Nancy, 65
Reeve, Christopher, 216
Robbins, Jerome, 21, 24, 84
Robert Joffrey Ballet, 28
Rolls Royce, 87
Royal Academy of Ballet, 21
Royal Ballet, 37, 79, 148
Royal Swedish, Ballet, 103
Ryukyu Islands, 57, 60
Sahara Desert, 139
St. Margarethen, 104
Sappington, Margo, 112, 123
Satinoff, Jeff, 184
School of American
  Ballet, 23, 27
Serrano, Lupe, 80, 95

Shah of Iran, 166
Shaw, Ted (Papa), 43
Schuman, 165
Singing in the Rain, 78
Skibine, George, 137
Sleeping Beauty, The,
  71, 135, 148, 178, 180
Smuin, Michael, 80
Sombert, Clair, 134
Spartacus, 161
Spoerli, Heinz, 168
Steps Studio, 164
Sternov, Rosa, 28
Stevenson, Ben, 147
Stuttgart Ballet, 169
Subways Are For Sleeping, 25
Sun Life of Canada
  Assurance Co., 195
Supremes, The, 83
Suzuki, 203
Swan Lake, 71, 80, 142,
  143, 145, 160, 194
Symphony in C, 73

Table Mountain, 151
Tamoxifen, 225
Tchaikovsky, 144, 152
Tchernichova, Elena, 131, 164
Temptations, The, 83
The Boston Globe, 190
The Dance Academy, 178, 202
The Lexington Health Club, 210
The Red Shoes, 81
The Wizard of Oz, 38
Thompson, Dorothy
   School of Dancing, 7
Tidewater Ballet, 186
Time Magazine, 34
Trailine, Boris, 159
Tudor, Anthony, 80, 82
United Nations, 207
United States
   Department of Defense, 44
University of Buffalo, 20
University of Massachusetts, 192
USO, 57
Vaganova, 132, 179
Valentino's, 26
Van Clef and Arpels, 26
Varna Ballet Competition, 112
Vasco de Gama, 153
Vietnam War, 44
Villella, Edward, 102
Virginia State Ballet, 173
Wagner, Richard, 169
Walker, Norman, 42, 108
Walpurgis Nacht, 24
Wells Theatre, 184
West Side Story, 21, 24, 25, 37
Williams, Ted, 193
Williams, Virginia, 39
Williamsville, Inn, The, 22
Wilson, Sallie, 80, 165
Who's Who in American
   Women, 207
World Airlines, 60
YMCA, 26
Youskevitch, Igor, 96
Zaraspe, Hector, 42
Zorba the Greek, 90

www.ingramcontent.com/pod-product-compliance
Lightning Source LLC
Chambersburg PA
CBHW071429150426
43191CB00008B/1090